Kathryn Graham
Sarah J. Saunders
Margaret C. Flower

Carol Birchmore Timney
Marilyn White-Campbell
Anne Zeidman Pietropaolo

Addictions Treatment for Older Adults: Evaluation of an Innovative Client-Centered Approach

D1571174

*Pre-publication
REVIEWS,
COMMENTARIES,
EVALUATIONS . . .*

" **T**his won\ scribes an innovative and successful treatment project for older people who have problems with alcohol or other drugs. The COPA (Community Older Persons Alcohol) Program was started in Toronto in 1983 by S. J. Saunders, a physician who recognized even at that time that alcohol and drug problems are not restricted to young people, and that when older people do have such problems they often manifest themselves in a variety of unexpected ways that make them difficult to detect and treat.

counter to most traditional addictions treatment programs which require abstinence as a criterion for admission, and believe that change can only occur when the client acknowledges and overcomes a substance abuse problem.

The very detailed descriptions provided by the authors of the variables measured, how they were measured, and how the authors overcame a variety of methodological problems, should encourage replication and further research regarding older people with substance abuse problems."

Virginia Carver, PhD
Senior Program Consultant,
Addiction Research Foundation,
Ottawa, Canada

"The authors have produced an up-to-date review of the problem of toxic abuse in the elderly with careful attention to each separate aspect: prevalence, phenomology, differential nosology, diagnostic challenges and, most importantly, the particular difficulties experienced in the therapeutic management of this specific population.

The text describes in detail the firsthand experience gained through the utilization of an original approach. All of the information the reader would like to know is there; from the way the program functions at a clinical level (including a number of very descriptive case summaries) to the criteria and method followed to assess its efficacy and efficiency. In fact, all the diagnostic instruments and rating scales developed in that program have been annexed to the text. This is a most useful publication: one that will benefit clinicians, researchers, and program planners. It will serve as a helpful reference in the library of every addiction worker and as an enlightening guide for anyone interested in working with the elderly."

J. C. Negrete, MD, FRCP
Professor of Psychiatry,
McGill University;
Director, Addictions Unit,
Montreal General Hospital

The Haworth Press, Inc.

Addictions Treatment for Older Adults

Evaluation of an Innovative Client-Centered Approach

New, Recent, and Forthcoming Titles:

Group Psychotherapy with Addicted Populations by Philip J. Flores

Shame, Guilt and Alcoholism: Treatment Issues in Clinical Practice by Ronald T. Potter-Efron

Neuro-Linguistic Programming in Alcoholism Treatment edited by Chelly M. Sterman

Cocaine Solutions: Help for Cocaine Abusers and Their Families by Jennifer Rice-Licare and Katherine Delaney-McLoughlin

Preschoolers and Substance Abuse: Strategies for Prevention and Intervention by Pedro J. Lecca and Thomas D. Watts

Chemical Dependency and Antisocial Personality Disorder: Psychotherapy and Assessment Strategies by Gary G. Forrest

Substance Abuse and Physical Disability edited by Allen W. Heinemann

Addiction in Human Development: Developmental Perspectives on Addiction and Recovery by Jacqueline Wallen

Addictions Treatment for Older Adults: Evaluation of an Innovative Client-Centered Approach by Kathryn Graham, Sarah J. Saunders, Margaret C. Flower, Carol Birchmore Timney, Marilyn White-Campbell, and Anne Zeidman Pietropaolo

Addictions Treatment for Older Adults
Evaluation of an Innovative Client-Centered Approach

Kathryn Graham, PhD
Sarah J. Saunders, MD
Margaret C. Flower, RN
Carol Birchmore Timney, MA
Marilyn White-Campbell, DGrt
Anne Zeidman Pietropaolo, BSW, BEd

The Haworth Press
New York • London • Norwood (Australia)

The Haworth Press, Inc., 10 Alice Street, Binghamton, NY 13904-1580

Library of Congress Cataloging-in-Publication Data

Addictions treatment for older adults : evaluation of an innovative client-centered approach / Kathryn Graham . . . [et al.].
    p. cm.
    Includes bibliographical references and index.
    ISBN 1-56024-857-2 (acid-free paper).
    1. Aged–Alcohol use. 2. Aged–Drug use. 3. Alcoholism–Treatment. 4. Drug abuse–Treatment. I. Graham, Kathryn Marie.
HV5138.A33 1994
362.29′18′0846–dc20
                                    93-29334
                                        CIP

CONTENTS

ABOUT THE AUTHORS

Kathryn Graham, PhD, is a scientist with the Addiction Research Foundation in London, Ontario, Canada. Over the past ten years, her research has involved evaluation of addictions treatment programs and systems with special focus on treatment of older adults, case management, and relapse prevention. She has published on these topics as well as on topics pertaining to evaluation methods. Her current research includes an evaluation of a community intervention to prevent and treat problems related to use of alcohol and prescription drugs by older adults and a line of research examining the social factors related to alcohol use and problems.

Sarah J. Saunders, MD, founder of the Community Older Persons Alcohol Program (COPA), is currently retired from the Addiction Research Foundation. While there, she was involved in the development of one of the first community outreach assessment and referral services in Ontario. As a staff physician, she worked in various capacities, including lecturing at the University of Toronto. During the past twenty years, Dr. Saunders has played a major role in education, program development, and research in the area of alcohol and drug use and misuse by older adults.

Margaret C. Flower, RN, has ten years of front line experience in addictions counseling and health education, working with government, hospitals, and social services. Currently, she is an assessment worker with Metro Addiction Assessment Referral Service in Toronto. She has presented workshops and seminars to health care professionals and published on substance abuse and the elderly.

Carol Birchmore Timney, MA, is Research Associate with the Addiction Research Foundation. She has been involved in research in the area of case management in the addictions treatment system and the impact of substance abuse on the family.

Marilyn White-Campbell, DGrt, is a consultant gerontologist and a primary care outreach worker with COPA. She has made many invited presentations on working with older people who have substance-related problems and on issues related to elder abuse. She has also been involved in several research projects relating to alcohol and drug use by older people.

Anne Zeidman Pietropaolo, BSW, BEd, completed a clinical internship at COPA and played a major role in the case study research conducted as part of the COPA evaluation. She is a teacher at the George Syme Community School in Toronto and a member of the City of York Board of Education.

Preface

This book describes the results of evaluation research conducted over several years at the Community Older Persons Alcohol (COPA) program. COPA is a program specifically designed for older adults who are experiencing problems related to the use of alcohol or other drugs. A variety of evaluation approaches were adopted since the program differed greatly from traditional addictions programs and the clients reflected a population usually not served by addictions treatment programs.

The program philosophy is that counselors can help people reduce substance abuse and improve other areas of their lives by allowing each person to determine his or her own treatment needs. Moreover, the program is unlike other addictions treatment programs in that clients of the program are not required to admit that they have an alcohol or drug problem in order to receive help. Although the treatment process typically includes counseling and education regarding the relationship between specific life problems and consumption of alcohol and drugs, the overall focus is holistic and driven by the needs of the client. The range of interventions is broad, often involving counseling in the person's home, accompanying the client to important appointments, and advocacy and coordination with other services and with the clients' family on behalf of the clients. A full description of the program and its rationale is provided in Chapters 1 and 2.

Evaluation of the COPA approach required considerable deviation from classical pre-test/post-test evaluation designs. In particular, the lack of a requirement for clients to admit to alcohol and drug problems presented unusual difficulties for evaluation. For many clients, a valid assessment of pre-treatment functioning only emerged as the client and counselor developed rapport over the course of the treatment process. Thus, since valid information only emerged through the treatment process, usual evaluation methods, such as using a no-treatment control group, were not possible. Therefore, assessing the extent that clients improved during treatment involved the use of several convergent methods of data collection. The flexible individualized approach to treatment also posed problems for evaluation. Again, the approach was to draw conclusions from the convergence of several methods. One method used to better understand the clients and the treatment process was the case study. Thirty-six studies were completed. There are presented in Chapter 3 to provide an overall sense of the nature of the clients, the program, and the recovery process. The methodological approach to the more quantitative aspects of the evaluation is described in Chapter 4.

The remainder of the book focuses on the findings of the evaluation. Chapters 5, 6, and 7 describe the characteristics of COPA clients and relate these findings to what is currently reported in the scientific literature about older substance abusers. Chapters 8, 9, and 10 describe how outcomes were measured, overall outcomes of the COPA program, and predictors of outcome. Again, these results are discussed in terms of the existing literature and the general implications of the findings. The final chapter (Chapter 11) summarizes the major findings and conclusions of the COPA evaluation.

Acknowledgements

Evaluation of the Community Older Persons Alcohol (COPA) Program took place over a number of years and benefited from contributions by many people. We cannot list everyone who contributed in some way, but would like to take this opportunity to express our appreciation to some of the major participants in the project.

During the early part of the project, Jim Shea was a counselor at COPA. Besides providing data from his client contacts, he also contributed his wisdom to refining the data collection methods. Jadzia Romaniec became part of the COPA study as an observer in our initial attempts to assess inter-rater reliability of the data we were collecting. Her suggestions improved the process and her observations helped us to find ways to keep the project on track. During most of this study, the administration of the project was done by Helen Carvalho. As secretary at COPA, she made clients feel comfortable, handled numerous crises on the telephone, and generally managed the heavy administrative burden of the evaluation. This included making sure the counselors completed their paperwork and organizing information to be sent to the researchers. She left COPA to work full-time on her Bachelor of Science degree.

Susan Miklejohn from the Community Occupational Therapists Association (COTA) was generous with her time in the early stages of the project. She was very helpful in refining the treatment approach. Queen Elizabeth Hospital (Toronto, Ontario) provided space and other types of support. Throughout the project, we received consistent support from the COPA Board and from the Addiction Research Foundation (ARF). In particular, this project could not have done without the support of Mario Faveri of the ARF. Cindy Smythe of the ARF read numerous drafts of this and other reports about COPA and provided helpful suggestions. Pamela Brett also provided helpful comments. Dr. Bruce Carruth (Series Editor) provided useful suggestions for improving this book, as did the technical editors at The Haworth Press. Barb Keogan, Sue Steinback, Wendy Rush, and Cindy Reid were able to meet high demands on their word processing expertise, both in the preparation of this book and in the production of compact data collection forms.

Also, a number of colleagues in the fields of addictions and gerontology took the time to provide helpful feedback on the typology of older alcohol abusers developed from the case studies (Chapter 3).

Finally, the most important contributors to acknowledge are the clients of COPA. Because the study was unobtrusive, most clients did not know they were contributing to research. Nevertheless, they were the ones who taught us about the subject of "alcohol and the elderly" and showed the counselors the kind of help that was needed and wanted. We are especially grateful to the clients who allowed an observer into their homes so that we could assess the reliability of the data we were collecting. The clients, their stories, and their spirit made the evaluation challenging (at times frustrating!) but, most of the time, a lot of fun.

Chapter 1

The Need for Addictions Treatment for the Elderly

Only in the past decade have the special needs of older persons who have alcohol or drug problems been given much consideration. This lack of attention to substance problems of older persons was partially attributable to the low problem rate estimated for this group on the basis of general population surveys. National surveys in the U.S. and Canada have indicated that older persons report the lowest rate of alcohol problems and the highest rate of abstinence compared to other adult age groups (Clark & Midanik, 1982; Health and Welfare Canada, 1990). In addition, illicit drug use is exceedingly rare among older adults (Health and Welfare Canada, 1990). Moreover, surveys of treatment programs have found that older persons are underrepresented in treatment populations (Rush & Tyas, 1990).

Nevertheless, substance use and abuse by older people has begun to receive more attention. This has occurred for several reasons. First, problem rates based on community surveys may underestimate the extent of the problem, since surveys usually exclude institutionalized elderly where problem rates seem to be higher (see review by Gomberg, 1982). Second, problem rates may be inaccurate because the framework for defining alcohol problems has tended to be based on the problems experienced by younger people (e.g., family problems, employment problems) rather than those types of problems more likely to be experienced by older alcohol abusers, such as inability to care for self and home, and memory or cognitive problems (Graham, 1986).

Third, it is well recognized that the human body's ability to absorb and eliminate alcohol and drugs deteriorates with aging.

Therefore, older persons may be more likely to experience problems from levels of alcohol use that typically would not cause problems for younger persons. Fourth, prescription drug use (including use of psychoactive prescription drugs) is highest among older people (Health and Welfare Canada, 1990). Prescription drugs may directly cause problems for the user (e.g., problem consequences, addiction), or these drugs may interact with alcohol, accentuating any effects of drinking. Finally, as will be described in Chapter 2, clinical primary care workers (e.g., physicians, public health nurses) began to express a need for strategies for dealing with older people experiencing alcohol and drug problems. Thus, despite the low prevalence rates indicated by general population surveys and surveys of treatment programs, greater attention began to be paid to the problem because of cases being encountered by families of older persons and by health and other professionals interacting with older persons.

The overall conclusion of recent literature reviews (Schonfeld & Dupree, 1990) is that alcohol and drug problems among older persons need to be addressed, despite the apparent low prevalence of such problems. As the population ages, even a small rate of problem use is likely to translate into increasingly larger numbers. In addition, there is some speculation that those who will become elderly in the near future are more likely to be drinkers and, therefore, more likely to have drinking problems, although the evidence is mixed as to whether drinking decreases with age (Adams et al., 1990; Busby et al., 1988; Glynn et al., 1984; Temple & Leino, 1989).

ADDICTIONS TREATMENT ISSUES PERTAINING TO OLDER ADULTS

There has been only a small amount of research on the treatment needs of older adults who have substance problems, or on the effectiveness of addictions treatment programs for older people. As the literature on treatment needs of older persons has grown, suggestions regarding treatment have been proposed based on identified characteristics of the target population. These suggestions have included: that treatment of older substance abusers requires knowledge of both alcoholism and aging and that the aged alcoholic is particularly likely to fall between the cracks of the support service network (Rathbone-McCuan et al., 1976); that the older alcoholic is usually hidden, and therefore it may be necessary to involve out-reach caseworkers in treatment (Duckworth & Rosenblatt, 1976); and that support services should exist for older alcoholics who cannot or do not want to be "cured" (Van de Vyvere, Hughes, & Fish, 1976). Other suggestions for treatment have been based on physicians' informal clinical experience with older persons who have alcohol problems. These include suggestions that there is a need for medical and supportive treatment; that treatment directed at social and psychological stresses is particularly useful (Droller, 1964; Rosin & Glatt, 1971; Zimberg, 1978a); and that service delivery needs to involve outreach, case-finding, and home-care (Zimberg, 1978b). Also on the basis of clinical experience (in a geriatric center), Rathbone-McCuan suggested that a comprehensive assessment is an important part of treatment (including case identification), and that community agencies need to work together in designating one resource for inpatient treatment and in providing ongoing case management (Rathbone-McCuan, 1982). Rathbone-McCuan also recommended that a suitable typology for helping the older problem drinker could be based on the presence or absence of (1) alcoholism or symptoms of problem drinking, (2) health problems, and (3) difficulties or inadequacies in the social network (Rathbone-McCuan & Bland, 1975).

A distinct issue that has emerged in the literature is whether there is a need for elder-specific treatment. While early views on the subject (based on clinical experience) promoted the need for special programs for older people who have substance problems, Hinrichsen (1984) surveyed staff in 40 alcoholism treatment programs in six states and found that the majority (84 percent) felt that age-segregated treatment was unnecessary. However, recent data suggest that those who receive elder-specific treatment remain in treatment longer and are more likely to complete treatment than those in mixed-age outpatient groups (Kofoed et al., 1987).

In sum, specific considerations for treating older substance abusers have received very little attention until recently. The prevailing views of those who have written on this topic include the following: that outreach is required, that age-specific programs may be desirable, and that non-confrontational individual or group approaches based on providing social and medical support are likely to be most useful. There is also some evidence that older alcoholics do at least as well in treatment as younger alcoholics (Carstensen, Rychtarik, & Prue, 1985; Hanson, 1988; Linn, 1978).

Chapter 2

The Development of the Community
Older Persons Alcohol (COPA) Program

The following is extracted from a recent paper by Graham, Saunders, and Flower (1990) and describes the background that led Dr. Sarah J. Saunders to establish the COPA project:

> In the late 1960s when I first started working in the field of addictions, the conclusion of the research literature was essentially that older people did not have alcohol problems. This view was partly based on the fact that very few people age 65+ ever entered an alcoholism treatment program and consequently were not visible to those persons in the alcoholism treatment field.
>
> Then, when I was invited to develop a treatment program for a group of actively drinking men, creating behavioral havoc in a large home for the aged, it seemed like an interesting challenge but a rather low priority. Fortunately, I had the time to respond. I was aware that Alcoholics Anonymous had been involved in the home for 18 months with all contact being totally refused by these residents. What evolved was a quasi-behavioral program that seemed to work after about 9 months—work in the sense that the behavior problems and frequency of intoxication dropped significantly (according to daily records of alcohol use and related behavior). Associated with this drop was a significant improvement in socializing skills and non-alcohol-related use of leisure time. At no time did the residents acknowledge a problem with their use of alcohol. This concept was important in the development of future programs.
>
> Over the next 8 years as this program was enlarged, I began receiving many requests from the community for assistance

with elderly alcohol abusers. I noted that most of these requests came from home caregivers. Consequently, I began making home visits with community health nurses to see if indeed there was a population of elderly alcoholics who were not being identified–there was!

Common themes that emerged were:

- most refused to leave the home for almost any reason
- many demonstrated problems related to alcohol use in every aspect of their lives
- most totally resisted any suggestion of formal treatment for alcoholism
- many identified needs that seemed to be quite different from those of younger alcoholics.

What I learned from this experience was that given the opportunity to resolve some of their more acceptable problems (health, housing), helping them make the link between these problems and their use of alcohol was also often possible. We found that working with people on other problems often seemed to lead to their reducing their alcohol consumption, although total abstinence occurred in only a few people. However, even without total abstinence, the majority of those persons visited seemed to improve significantly in terms of living arrangements, health, non-alcohol-related socializing and leisure activities, as well as reduced alcohol consumption. We also found that because of the multiplicity and variety of lifestyle problems, many other agencies and services needed to be involved in the therapeutic process.

We seemed to have identified a hitherto unrecognized population of elderly alcohol abusers, and had developed a means whereby treatment was possible and apparently effective. By January 1981 I was receiving requests to develop a formal treatment program for elderly persons living in their own homes. A planning committee was formed that included representatives from all the major gerontological resources in Toronto as well as the Addiction Research Foundation (ARF). The concept for the COPA program was developed in May 1981. When taking into account all the themes identified in the earlier project, the new program bore little resemblance to existing alcohol treatment programs either in the treatment goals, methodology or program content. (pp. 197-198)

In 1983, the Community Older Persons Alcohol (COPA) Program was established in West Toronto. The program was developed specifically to meet the needs of hard-to-reach older people who have alcohol or drug problems and was structured on three major principles: (1) that outreach should be provided where appropriate to older people who have substance problems, rather than assuming (as with traditional addictions programs) that persons should come *to* the program; (2) that it was not necessary for clients of the program to acknowledge substance problems in order for meaningful change to take place (again, a principle in direct opposition to traditional addictions treatment approaches); and (3) that one important goal of addictions treatment for older persons is to maintain the independent living of these persons in the community (by linking them with necessary community supports).

For the purpose of this book, Margaret Flower (the first director of COPA) provided the following reminiscences regarding the delivery of the program in its early days:

Travelling uncharted areas, we had no "clinical model." We went with hope, learn on the job, do no harm, and improvise. What I *think* we did was:

a. Responded immediately to the problem(s) identified by the client–regardless of its origin (i.e., even if not directly related to substance abuse), building trust, rapport, providing immediate support, and providing case management. This was done with "high intensity empathy!"

b. Kept clear definitions of the client's goals versus "our" goals–my feeling is that much of this was done at staff meetings through case consultation. These meetings provided a forum for keeping perspective on clients' strengths and achievements (small goals) and ensuring that our motives were in the clients' best interests. Since the program was innovative and we were not able to measure our work against existing programs, these meetings helped to affirm that we were on the right track.

c. Some of the issues that we had to deal with included: What would happen when we disengaged–would the client relapse? Did we recognize our limitations? How could we involve other supports (e.g., other agencies, families)? Probably treatment is the wrong word for our approach. What we tried to do was introduce a new element for the client–*choice*.

"Accepting" the client and being there for them became an actuality, not just a phrase. It started with visiting homes, often in total squalor (reflecting not just the addiction limiting the individual, but often physical, mental and emotional barriers to care). Being non-judgmental was crucial. We had to be open to the possibility that the living circumstances were the free choice of the individual. Assessment included the client's satisfaction with the existing lifestyle.

It was necessary that we recognize the strengths and past achievements of the client and verbalize this recognition to the client. It was with some difficulty that we developed the patience and skills to elicit this information from clients *and* to recognize its value as part of treatment.

Doing the conventional aspects of treatment were relatively easy: assessing needs, prioritizing needs, and facilitating help and support from agencies and family. These aspects of the job tended to provide us with a sense of accomplishment and satisfaction–that we had "improved" someone's situation. On the other hand, to be prepared to allow the client to determine what treatment was necessary/acceptable/least intrusive was a more frustrating process. Accepting that no treatment was necessary or wanted was a scary experience.

Generally, the treatment, then as now, consisted of an extensive period of assessment and engaging the client in treatment followed by a variety of actions, including support, practical help, referral, problem solving, and sometimes confrontation. In the following section, the courses of treatment for two COPA clients are described in detail to demonstrate the application of the COPA philosophy.

THE COURSE OF TREATMENT
FOR TWO COPA CLIENTS

The following sections describe in detail the course of treatment for two COPA clients. First, an overall summary of each case is provided, followed by a treatment summary where each contact with the client during treatment is described, as well as other events where applicable. Each treatment summary is fairly complete, but may underestimate the number of contacts with the client, as phone calls and other brief contacts with the client (e.g., meeting on the street) were often not documented.

These cases are also included in the typology (Chapter 3): the first client described here appears as Case 10, and the second client is Case 15. These cases were chosen to demonstrate the variability and complexity of older substance abusers and their problems. They also demonstrate the flexible approach to treatment taken by the COPA counselors.

Client 1: Case Summary

At referral, this 64-year-old man was spending all his time in his rented room eating very little, and in deteriorating physical health. He was profoundly depressed, isolated, and inactive. Because of his poor health and lack of mobility, he was not drinking, but according to the community nurse who referred him, the client had a long history of alcohol abuse (possibly skid row alcoholic lifestyle).

Initially, the client was very passive and did not respond to program efforts to improve his circumstances. After a couple of months, he appeared to welcome the emotional support and practical assistance and developed a close relationship with the program counselor. During the early phases of treatment, the focus was on improving the client's immediate housing, financial, physical, emotional, and nutritional problems. After his initial crisis was resolved, the areas of focus for intervention began to include reducing alcohol consumption and promoting better social/leisure activities, better care of self and home, and appropriate use of medications. During aftercare, the program worker provided ongoing support and practical assistance to the client where needed. During treatment, he was seen over a period of 29 months at 60 home visits, several chance meetings, and several contacts to help him pick up furnishings. In addition, there were numerous telephone contacts with or about him. During treatment, the client was seen by a visiting nurse, a community health clinic, Meals-on-Wheels, welfare, housing authorities, a GP, a seniors' information center, the Mission, and a public trustee.

Over the course of his treatment, the client exhibited improvement in assertiveness and self-esteem. Although the initial goal for the client was to find a good boarding home, by the end of treatment the client was maintaining independent living in his own apartment (obtained through subsidized housing) and he was taking good care of himself and his apartment, eating regularly, getting exercise, and engaging in satisfying social activities and recreation. Although the client continued to drink throughout the program, he was able to reduce his intake to a level that did not appear to be detrimental to his physical health or his well-being in other life areas. He had several relapses into heavier drinking during his treatment, but by the time he was discharged these bouts had been reduced.

At the follow-up stage of the research (about two and a half years after discharge), the client was contacted by telephone. He reported that he was doing fairly well and managing to live on his own in an apartment. He had problems with arthritis that hampered his activity somewhat, but was able to engage in some activities and was in fair spirits. He reported that his current alcohol consumption was about 12 beers on weekends. He felt that the program had provided a great deal of help and mentioned the counselor by name and how helpful he had been.

Client 1: Treatment Summary

[Counselor's actions or responses are in brackets.]

1. *Initial home visit with public health nurse.* Client has no money, no food, and no cooking facilities. Meals-on-Wheels (three

times/week) seems to be his only food. He has been losing weight, experiencing blackouts, and says he has no feeling in his legs below the knees. [Assessment.]

2. *Home visit (8 days later).* Client is still eating poorly and experiencing vivid dreams, possibly hallucinations. He is depressed and hopeless. [Assessment.]

3. *Home visit by COPA counselor with a physician (2 days later).* Client has been abstinent for several weeks due to lack of money. He has fits (possibly epilepsy) and frightening dreams. He is nervous and isolated. [Recommendations: (1) he should have accommodation where he is provided three meals/day; (2) medical check-up as soon as possible; and (3) psychogeriatric assessment.]

4. *Home visit (5 days later).* Situation is unchanged and client refuses to do anything.

5. *Telephone call (2 days later).* Client says food from Meals-on-Wheels has not been delivered. [Counselor offered to bring him food.]

6. *Home visit (same day).* Meals-on-Wheels had arrived. Client was cheerful and had washed his face and combed his hair. [Counselor brought client food and commented positively on his appearance.]

7. *Home visit (6 days later).* Client is very concerned about his health, but he also has a defeatist attitude and refuses to address problems. [Counselor and client discussed client's boyhood.]

[Case notes: Referral has been made for psychogeriatric assessment. The public health nurse is going to contact client's sister to see if she will provide some support.]

8. *Home visit (20 days later).* Client is in poor physical health. He is defeatist about changing accommodation or dealing with health problems. [Counselor made suggestions about alternate accommodations.]

9. *Home visit with second COPA counselor who will be taking over case (28 days later).* Client is still not drinking and health is still poor. He is lethargic, depressed, and hopeless. He perked

up greatly when he found that the second counselor was from the same city as he was. He was washed and dressed although hair not combed. His economic situation seems stable but blinds, TV, and armchair missing from room (apparently taken by landlady). [Counselor actions: advice, problem solving, empathy, seeking information, and monitoring. The new counselor offered to help him find new accommodation.]

10. *Home visit (6 days later).* Client reported that he had six beers on the previous Saturday. He complained about legs and weakness (especially, difficulty walking to store and carrying beer!). He also complained about bowels, and that his landlady cashes his welfare check and keeps too much. He was in fairly good spirits but still expressed a defeatist attitude. [Counselor discouraged drinking and encouraged more walking and to take his vitamins; he also advised and encouraged the client to move, and suggested that the client should cash the welfare check himself.]

11. *Home visit (7 days later).* Client has been abstinent and has been walking. He complained of tired legs, ringing in his ears, and poor vision (symptoms he had reported previously). He is emotionally better and his cognitive status is good. Personal care and nutrition are better, and he has worked out some problems with his landlady. [Counselor reinforced abstinence, suggested seeing a doctor, and encouraged client to continue buying food. Other actions: listening, empathy.]

   [Case notes (next day): Psychogeriatric assessment not done because when counselor and assessment worker went to his home he would not answer the door.]

12. *Home visit (6 days later).* Client has been abstinent and shows good self-care. He is more positive–initiated conversation about moving. He described his skid row past to the counselor, and the client and counselor went for a walk. [The counselor reinforced self-care, discussed options for moving, and encouraged the client to move. Other actions: listening, empathy, monitoring.]

13. *Chance meeting (7 days later).* The client said his legs were sore and he had lost more weight (but he walked quite far with

the worker). He was in good spirits and very alert. He said he walks every day and that he knows lots of people on the street, although he does not talk to them. He said that he was thinking about picking up an application for Metro Housing, as someone had told him the rent was reasonable. [The counselor told the client that he looked like he had put on weight and was walking well. He accompanied him to the information center to pick up an application for Metro Housing and encouraged him to proceed with obtaining better housing.]

14. *Chance meeting (7 days later).* [Before bumping into the client, the counselor had been to the client's room, where he spoke with the landlady. The client's room had been divided in half, with the other half rented to another person!] The client reported that he had consumed several beers in the past week. He reported trouble with his eyes and stomach. He also indicated that he was not happy with the landlady subdividing his room. [The counselor confronted the client that money spent on beer could not be used for food. He accompanied the client to the doctor to make an appointment for a check-up. He also advised and encouraged the client to move.]

15. *Home visit (14 days later).* The client reported that he had had several drinks in the past week. He had been to the doctor and several of his health concerns had been addressed. He was walking well and in good emotional health with good mental status. He mentioned that his brother had invited him to his cottage. He completed the Metro Housing form with the counselor. [The counselor advised the client to continue limiting his drinking. He reinforced the client's efforts to improve his health and helped the client complete the Metro Housing form.]

16. *Home visit (7 days later).* Client is about the same. He wants to move and may move in with some friends. [The counselor had been exploring options on the client's behalf. Other actions: advice, monitoring, empathy.]

17. *Home visit (7 days later).* Client has been consuming alcohol during the past week. He has some physical complaints and has made appointments at a health center. The landlady owes him

money. [The counselor encouraged action in health area. Other actions: listening, monitoring.]

18. *Home visit (2 days later).* Client reported that his legs have been worse although he has been taking his medications. He was agitated and talkative. He does not want to move in with his friend because the friend is a heavy drinker. He went with the counselor to see the landlady and arranged to pay by the week while he is looking for a new accommodation. [Counselor accompanied client to see landlady. Other actions: empathy, encouragement, monitoring.]

[Case notes (6 days later): Went to see client but the landlady said he had moved.]

19. *Home visit (12 days after previous home visit).* The client has moved into a three-bedroom apartment that he shares with another man and woman. He said that he had had a few beers occasionally. His legs have been worse and he did not keep his appointment with the urologist at the health center. He said he was eating well. [Encouraged the client to make another appointment at the health center. Other actions: listening, empathy.]

20. *Home visit (8 days later).* The client has been drinking with apartment-mate, and his drinking has increased. His health complaints are less, but he has not rescheduled at the health center. His sister visits often, and his emotional and mental status is good. He and the counselor completed a new form for Metro Housing. [Helped complete Metro Housing Form. Other actions: empathy, monitoring.]

21. *Home visit (7 days later).* The client has not been drinking lately because of lack of money. He talked with the counselor about his heavy drinking in the past. He has not been taking any medications. His emotional status and mental status are good. He has found out that there is a long wait with Metro Housing. [The counselor confronted the client about the heavy drinking by the friend who shares the apartment. The counselor also made the connection to the client between the client's reduced

alcohol consumption and his current better health and general well-being. He encouraged the client to go to the doctor.]

22. *Home visit (10 days later).* The client had been drinking. He is in good spirits and his economic situation is somewhat better. He told the counselor that Metro Housing was supposed to visit but had not. [The counselor was seeking information from the client about housing and monitoring. He told the client that Metro Housing had probably sent someone to his old address. The counselor called Metro Housing for the client and rescheduled an appointment.]

23. *Home visit (11 days later).* The client reported that he had been drinking 24 beers/week. He told the counselor that the Metro Housing worker had visited him the day before and said that he was not appropriate for an apartment, and he should go to a Home for the Aged. [The counselor cautioned the client that he should not increase his alcohol consumption. The counselor said he would call Metro Housing for clarification.]

24. *Home visit (7 days later).* The client was evasive about how much alcohol he had been consuming ("a few"), but he had drunk a bottle of wine the previous day. He exhibited some memory impairment. He completed an application form for a group home through Metro Housing. [The counselor discouraged heavy consumption and helped the client complete the application form for the group home. The counselor advised and encouraged the client to go to the doctor for a medical exam and X ray.]

25. *Home visit (7 days later).* The client reported that he "sipped away" at "a few." He said that drinking helped pass the time. His legs are bad but he had not been to a doctor. He is not in a hurry to move from the apartment. He appeared slightly confused. [The counselor cautioned the client that he should watch his consumption because any amount could be damaging to his health, and he encouraged the client to take up other leisure activities. The counselor encouraged the client to go to the doctor so that his application for the group home could be processed, and he suggested that the client's current housing was not very good because of his heavy-drinking friend.]

26. *Home visit (14 days later).* The client has been drinking 12 beers/day. His legs are worse but he has not been to the doctor. When asked, he said he did not intend to go. [The counselor gave advice and helped in problem-solving about alternative leisure activities. The counselor continued to monitor the situation and suggested that the client go to the doctor.]

27. *Home visit (7 days later).* The client is still drinking heavily, although he talked of quitting for the winter because of icy roads and bad weather. His legs have been bad. He talked with the counselor about people he knew at the Mission. He said that Metro Housing wanted a reference from his previous landlady–which was probably not possible. [The counselor warned the client about the effects of his drinking on his health (e.g., legs). He reinforced the idea of the client quitting for the winter and encouraged the client to keep his legs up. The counselor agreed with the client that the landlady would not give a reference and said that he (the counselor) would call Metro Housing and explain.]

28. *Home visit (7 days later).* The client is worried about his legs and has decided to quit drinking. He is not getting along well with his friend in the apartment. Metro Housing was insisting that he had to get a reference. [The counselor encouraged abstinence, suggested that the client take his medications, and encouraged the client to go to the doctor.]

29. *Home visit (7 days later).* The client said he drank a bottle of wine the previous night because of pain in his foot. He has been to the doctor for an X ray and blood tests and has another appointment scheduled. [The counselor suggested that drinking was not a good solution for pain and confronted the client about the effects of his drinking. The counselor reinforced the client's medical action and encouraged the client to have the doctor complete the form for the group home.]

    [Case notes: The counselor wrote a letter to Metro Housing providing a reference for the client.]

30. *Home visit (7 days later).* The client had consumed a few beers because he was bored. He had been to the doctor and had the forms completed. He was pleased that the counselor had sent a

reference to Metro Housing. [The counselor suggested that the client use other means to deal with boredom. Other actions: empathy, monitoring, advice.]

31. *Home visit (15 days later).* The client has been drinking since last contact. He said his legs hurt from walking too much. He has a new prescription from the doctor for edema and hypertension, and had been going to the doctor regularly. He is excited about plans for Metro Housing. [The counselor made the connection between alcohol use and painful legs. Other actions: empathy, monitoring, reinforcement for medical compliance.]

32. *Home visit (7 days later).* The client's health is better and he has been receiving regular treatment from the doctor. He wants to get a cane. His income has increased as he is now eligible for old age pension (which is more than welfare). He had some questions about the group home. [The counselor reinforced medical compliance and said he would look into getting a cane for the client. He suggested that the client contact Metro Housing about his questions about the group home.]

33. *Home visit (12 days later).* The client has been drinking a little and taking less medication than prescribed. His legs have been better. He had been interviewed by a Metro Housing worker for group home, but he told her that he did not want to go into a group home. He asked the counselor for materials on Homes for the Aged. [The counselor provided listening and monitoring, encouraged compliance with medications, and encouraged the client to make a decision about housing.]

34. *Home visit (2 days later).* The client has physical health problems and seems a bit confused. He had refused the group home and said he wanted his own apartment. [The counselor advised the client to rest his legs and encouraged medical compliance. The counselor advised the client to reapply to Metro Housing for an apartment, and engaged in a problem-solving discussion about housing.]

35. *Home visit (14 days later).* The client has been drinking occasionally and is doing well in all areas. He had refused an apartment with Ontario Housing because the apartment was too far away. He had asked them to call back in April with something

closer. He had had a good visit with his sister. [Listening, empathy, monitoring, reinforcement.]

36. *Home visit (7 days later).* The client has been drinking two to four drinks daily but is doing very well. His emotional health and mental health are excellent. The rent on his apartment (with his two friends) has been raised, but he plans to stay where he is for now. [The counselor monitored the client's status. The client will be put on ongoing support with the frequency of visits reduced to every two weeks.]

37. *Home visit (14 days later).* The client drinks occasionally but is doing very well in all areas. [Listening, empathy, advice, monitoring, reinforcement.]

38. *Home visit (21 days later).* The client is still drinking and had a fall three days before because he had drunk too much. Otherwise, he is doing very well and taking better care of himself. [Listening, empathy, monitoring, mild confrontation about drinking, reminded client of doctor's appointment.]

39. *Home visit (14 days later).* The client is doing very well. He has new shoes and is going out every day. [Listening, empathy.]

40. *Home visit (14 days later).* The client is doing very well. He has been offered an apartment by Ontario Housing and plans to take it. [The client's new apartment is outside of COPA's catchment area, but the counselor will stay with him through the transition. The counselor provided advice and problem solving concerning the move, suggesting that the client obtain moving expenses from welfare, etc.]

41. *Home visit (21 days later).* The client is doing very well although he is vague about his alcohol consumption. Whatever amount he is drinking does not seem to be interfering with his functioning. [The counselor engaged client in problem solving about whether to change doctors when he moves, etc. Other actions: empathy, encouragement, monitoring.]

42. *Home visit (1 month later).* The client's apartment-mate reported that the client drinks frequently but paces himself so that he never runs out of money and has enough food. The client is doing well and his finances are good. [Actions: problem solving

about the move–counselor told client that he would help him set up his apartment with whatever he needs. Other actions: empathy, monitoring, seeking information.]

43. *Home visit (14 days later).* Client is doing well. [Empathy, education (about resting legs), monitoring, reinforcement.]

44. *Home visit at client's new apartment (10 days later).* Client is doing very well and has been to visit his sister. [Empathy, monitoring.]

45. *Home visit (next day).* [Counselor brought client some bedding.]

46. *Home visit (13 days later).* Client has been drinking but is doing very well. [The counselor confronted the client a little about his drinking. Other action: empathy.]

47. *Home visit (14 days later).* Client is doing very well, but the apartment is not as clean as usual. [The counselor advised the client to get a broom and a mop. Other action: monitoring.]

48. *Home visit and trip to pick up furniture (10 days later).* Client is doing very well and his apartment is very clean. [The counselor helped the client pick out and transport furniture. Monitoring.]

49. *Home visit (11 days later).* Client is drinking occasionally. He is doing very well, and taking good care of himself and his living quarters. His nutrition is okay and his leisure activity is satisfactory. [Monitoring.]

50. *Home visit (16 days later).* The client is doing very well. He had visited with his sister ("fun"). His income has increased, and he plans to buy a TV. He has a minor problem with his eye. [The counselor suggested he go to the doctor about his eye. Other actions: empathy, monitoring.]

51. *Home visit (1 month later).* The client is doing very well. He discussed various plans for his apartment, including getting a phone. [Counselor will go with client to obtain phone. Other actions: empathy, monitoring.]

52. *Accompanied client to get phone (3 days later).* [The counselor explained to the client the method of payment and installment procedures.]

53. *Telephone contact (25 days later).* Client is doing well and was very chatty.

54. *Home visit (1 month later).* Client is doing well although there were about 50 empty beer bottles in his cupboard. Also, he had been banned from a large downtown mall for excessive loitering. He had purchased a new comforter and pillow. [Advice, monitoring; offered help, if needed.]

55. *Telephone contact (7 days later).* Social call from client.

56. *Accompanied client to pick up table and chairs at Mission (10 days later).* Client is doing very well and has purchased a new winter coat.

57. *Chance meeting (9 days later).* Chit-chat.

58. *Home visit 5 days before Christmas (17 days later).* Client is doing very well and having positive contacts with family. [Empathy, monitoring.]

59. *Accompanied client to buy a TV (17 days later).* Client is doing very well, although many empty beer bottles were visible. [The counselor helped the client order cable service for the TV.]

60. *Home visit (14 days later).* The client is doing well, but not as well as previously. His speech was a little slurred and he was apparently drinking two to six drinks/day. [Advice, empathy, encouragement, monitoring. The counselor will increase frequency of contacts for short term.]

61. *Home visit (14 days later).* The client is doing well, but a bit depressed. He expressed bitterness about the past ("starved on welfare") and about how long he waited to have his own apartment. He has been drinking daily. His speech was slurred and hygiene was poorer than normal. [The counselor provided empathy and monitoring. He also confronted the client about his drinking and connected the client's drinking with his recent weight gain.]

62. *Home visit (15 days later).* The client is doing better. [Empathy, reinforcement, monitoring.]

63. *Home visit (21 days later).* The client is doing very well. He saw a table at a flea market and asked the counselor to accompany him to look at it. [Empathy, monitoring.]

64. *Home visit (1 month later).* The client is doing well but has cuts above his eyes. He denies falls. [The counselor helped the client fix his table and bed. Other actions: empathy, encouragement, monitoring.]

[Case notes from COPA staff meeting: The client is doing well. He has some swelling in his ankles that the counselor thinks is from alcohol consumption, but the client believes is from too much walking. He telephones the COPA office frequently. He will be monitored once a month for a while.]

65. *Home visit (1 month visit).* The client is doing fair and has been to see the doctor. He appears to have increased drinking. His speech is mildly impaired and he complained of increased pain and cramps in his legs. [The counselor provided confrontation and education about alcohol consumption and its effects on his legs. Other actions: advice, empathy, encouragement, monitoring.]

66. *Chance meeting (18 days later).* The client is doing well.

67. *Telephone contact (2 days later).* The client called the worker. He was drunk and fell while talking on the phone. [The counselor advised him to go to bed.]

68. *Home visit (6 days later).* The client has been drinking although not as heavily as before. He thinks he should cut down on his drinking. He has some physical health problems, but his emotional and mental status are good. [The counselor confronted the client about his drinking and reinforced his plan to cut down. He helped the client set goals regarding his health. Other actions; empathy, encouragement, monitoring.]

69. *Boat trip for COPA clients (1 month later).* The client is doing well.

70. *Home visit (18 days later).* The client is doing very well. [Client discharged.]

71. *Follow-up contact by researcher doing case studies (25 months later).* The client reported drinking 12 beers each weekend, but

he has been managing fairly well, living on his own, and in fairly good spirits and health.

Client 2: Case Summary

The client was a 59-year-old woman. She had a long history of housing instability, low income (single mother on welfare), and binge drinking. At the time she entered treatment, she was manic-depressive with symptoms *not* well controlled. Her binges seemed to coincide with the extremes of her mood swings. She was in poor health, very isolated, and very inactive. At the time of referral, the client had been recently discharged from the hospital and was still very ill with digestive and bowel problems, possibly related to drinking. Other life areas that seemed to have been negatively affected by her drinking were: her relationship with her daughter, housing, moods, nutrition, and ability to care for herself. When drinking, she sometimes became quite ill, her personal appearance deteriorated, she was unable to comply with her medications regime, and she sometimes became unruly and verbally abusive. During treatment she binged twice. The only information on consumption during these binges was that one binge consisted of two bottles of wine.

The client was referred to COPA by her daughter, who was afraid that the mother would return to drinking after discharge from the hospital. The client acknowledged her alcohol problem and felt that she needed help from COPA to reduce her drinking. She had attended AA off and on for many years and had been abstinent for up to nine months at one time. Treatment focused on helping to stabilize her functioning in housing, physical health, and emotional health (i.e., manic-depressive symptoms); encouraging and reinforcing the client's effort at abstinence; and emotional support and referrals during times of crisis. The client was in the program for five months (at which point she moved out of the catchment area). During treatment of the client, the COPA worker made 11 home visits, three visits to the client in the hospital, plus six telephone contacts with the client and with other agencies concerning the client. In addition to counselling support, the worker took the client to the hospital, found a new boarding home for the client, helped the client fill out application forms, mediated between the client and the staff at the boarding home, educated boarding home staff about the need for the client to take her medications, and arranged the client's transportation to AA at her new location. Although initially she had experienced some crises relating to her binges (illness, disruptive behavior at her boarding home), she eventually reduced her drinking, improved her appearance, and improved her relationship with her daughter. After being in treatment for just over three months, she was admitted to the psychiatric ward of a hospital because of her manic-depressive disorder. From the hospital, she was discharged to a rest home outside of Toronto. During treatment, she received services from a psychiatric ward of a general hospital, an addictions hospital emergency ward, a GP, a mental health clinic, and AA.

At the follow-up stage of the research (approximately a year and a half after discharge from COPA), the client was contacted by phone. She was still living in the rest home and liked it there. Although she does not go out much, she socializes with residents at the rest home. She reported that her health was generally good and the relationship with her daughter was improving. She was slightly depressed, but her medications seemed to be stabilizing her fairly well. She reported that she had been abstinent since she left COPA and that she has no desire to drink. She felt that the program had been helpful, but could not say what, in particular, had been helpful. She felt the most important factor in her recovery was her move out of the city.

Client 2: Treatment Summary

[Counselor's actions or responses are in brackets.]

1. *Initial visit (home).* Client was recently discharged from the hospital. She is in poor health and has very poor housing. She exhibited flat affect. [Assessment, listening, empathy, encouragement.]

2. *Home visit (7 days later).* Client was feeling ill with diarrhea but did not want to go to the hospital. [The counselor offered to take the client to the hospital, and confirmed that the client had an appointment with a housing worker.]

3. *Accompanied client to hospital (5 days later).* The client is still ill and was shaking. She had two bottles of wine over the weekend. She complained that her "nerves were bad," and she wants to move immediately. [The counselor took the client to the health clinic and obtained a referral to the medical unit of an addictions hospital. She stayed with the client until the client was admitted overnight.]

[Case notes: The counselor found an appropriate boarding home for the client, and the client was discharged from the addictions hospital the next day and went to the boarding home.]

4. *Home visit (at boarding home) (2 days later).* Client has been abstinent the past few days. She was in a good mood and had been socializing with the other residents. [The counselor helped the client complete the information form for the boarding home. Other actions: listening, empathy.]

5. *Home visit (5 days later).* The client has been abstinent and has greatly improved her personal appearance. She was elated and extremely talkative. She had had to go to emergency at the psychiatric hospital for medication for her nerves, but had canceled her doctor's appointment at the addictions hospital. [The counselor suggested that the client needed a budget to manage money. Other actions: reinforcement, monitoring, listening, empathy.]

6. *Home visit (6 days later).* The client is still abstinent. It was the client's birthday and she was depressed. [The counselor encouraged the client to tell the doctor about her depression. Other actions: listening, empathy.]

7. *Home visit (11 days later).* The client is still abstinent and is satisfied with the boarding home, but she is concerned about money. [The counselor drew up a budget plan with the client, and will call welfare to arrange a change of address and purchase of new glasses for the client.]

8. *COPA Christmas Open House (3 days later).* The client was attentive, looked well, and interacted well.

9. *Home visit (5 days later).* The client is abstinent and looking well. She reported that her relationship with her daughter is improving. [Reinforcement, monitoring.]

10. *Home visit (7 days later).* The client appears to be quite manic. She plans to spend Christmas with her daughter. [Monitoring.]

11. *Home visit (7 days later).* The boarding home staff reported that the client has been binging and very disruptive. The client was weepy and upset. She told the counselor that she stole $60 from another resident and was drinking due to loneliness. She is very angry with the staff. [The counselor provided listening, empathy, reassurance, and acceptance of the client. The counselor mediated between the staff and the client and educated both regarding the client's need to take her medications regularly.]

12. *Hospital visit (7 days later).* Client is in a hospital psychiatric ward. She is still manic and very distracted. She is angry at the boarding home staff and does not want to return. [Listening, empathy, monitoring.]

13. *Hospital visit (2 days later).* Client is calmer and her appearance has improved. She may move into a new rooming house. [Reinforcement, monitoring.]

14. *Hospital visit (5 days later).* The client is stable but the doctor wants her in supportive housing. [Monitoring.]

    [Case notes (9 days later): The client was discharged from the hospital to a rest home. Case notes (4 days later): The director of the rest home phoned COPA to say that the client was not "fitting in well." The counselor will visit the rest home the next day. Case notes (the next day): The client has been transferred to another rest home in a small town. The worker will phone the client and arrange a visit.]

15. *Telephone contact (7 days later).* Client is unhappy at new residence. [Monitoring.]

16. *Home visit (2 days later).* Client looks well and reports that the food is good, the staff are nice, and the house is nice, but she still wants to move. [The counselor arranged for the client's transportation and attendance at AA and took the client out for coffee. Other actions: listening, goal setting, problem solving.]

[Client was discharged following this visit as she is out of catchment area.]

17. *Follow-up phone call (18 months later).* Client is abstinent and doing fairly well.

A GENERAL DESCRIPTION OF THE COPA TREATMENT APPROACH

The Community Older Persons Alcohol Program (COPA) is an outreach program specifically designed to meet the needs of older persons in the community who are experiencing alcohol and/or drug related problems. In providing assistance to these clients, every effort is made to maintain them in their homes and reach an improved state of physical and emotional well-being, including a reduction or elimination of their alcohol and/or drug dependence. (Taken from COPA Program description, 1992)[1]

Treatment at COPA is divided into three main stages:

1. assessment
2. active treatment
3. maintenance/aftercare

Although these are conceptually distinct phases, in practice they tend to overlap and intermingle. For example, assessment is a necessary primary stage usually conducted over a period of four weeks, but it is also an ongoing process that occurs throughout treatment. Conversely, treatment maintenance is the final stage involving infrequent supportive contact that can return to more intensive treatment during times of crisis.

Length of treatment and the time spent in each stage vary depending on the client's needs and strengths. For example, the entire treatment program for a recently widowed person who is misusing

---

1. For a more detailed description of the COPA approach, see Saunders et al., 1992.

alcohol for the first time may consist of only a few sessions of education on the effects of alcohol or on alcohol-drug interactions. On the other hand, a long-term alcohol abuser may need a year or more to develop a lifestyle that does not include heavy alcohol use, and to resolve the many sequelae of long-term alcohol abuse. This may include lengthy assessment (because of the many problem areas), lengthy treatment (to change highly practiced behaviors), and longer maintenance or support (to consolidate gains). Some of the principles of treatment at COPA include proceeding at the client's pace, and helping the client to replace the role of alcohol in his or her life with something more healthy. The following sections describe in more detail the various aspects of treatment at COPA.

Assessment

Assessment has several objectives that are crucial to treatment:

- introducing the COPA program and engaging the client in treatment
- identifying the client's problem areas that need to be addressed, as well as the client's strengths that can be drawn upon to address problems
- preparing a treatment plan with the client
- identifying any crises that should be addressed immediately

Engaging the Client in Treatment

Since COPA specifically targets clients who are unwilling to engage in traditional addictions treatment, the initial contacts with the client are crucial and must be handled with sensitivity. If possible, it is useful to have the referring person accompany the COPA counselor on initial contacts with the client. The client is told that the COPA counselor is visiting because someone has expressed concern about the client's drinking or drug use, but it is made clear to the client that the philosophy of the COPA program is to help the client with the problems that *the client* identifies. If the client's main concerns are loneliness or housing or money, these are the areas addressed by the worker. Although the counselor attempts to obtain information about drinking and prescription drug use, no pressure is put on a client who is reluctant to discuss these topics. The topic of substance use is approached tactfully with probing questions designed to make the client feel comfortable and accepted when describing their patterns of use. Nevertheless, some clients will not provide this information but will still accept help from and be accepted into the COPA program.

This subtle approach is contrary to the prevailing wisdom regarding addictions treatment. It is usually argued that treatment can work only if a client is willing to admit to and confront his or her drinking or drug use problems. Yet, this nonconfrontational approach has worked very well with the majority of COPA clients. Several aspects of the approach seem to contribute to its success. First, addressing other life areas nearly always identifies the role of alcohol or drug abuse in the occurrence or the maintenance of problems in these areas. When this becomes apparent to a client, sometimes he or she changes the substance-using behavior (without ever discussing his or her consumption), and sometimes this leads the client to begin to work with the COPA counselor to address problem substance use. A second way this approach seems to work is through the development of a trusting relationship with the COPA counselor. This relationship seems to facilitate the client addressing substance problems that he or she really wanted to address but did not know how. The empathy and support from the counselor can also provide the client with hope and reassurance that he or she can actually stop or reduce drinking or drug use.

Identifying Problem Areas and Strengths

Identifying problem areas and strengths is also an important aspect of assessment. While a comprehensive assessment is usually considered a necessary part of all addictions treatment, it is particularly crucial for older alcohol and drug abusers. First, the goals of the program are more than just changing substance using behavior–the goals include improving the person's overall well-being and helping to maintain independent living. Second, the nonconfrontational approach adopted by COPA is inconsistent with focusing primarily on substance abuse. Third, because of the particular vulnerability of older people and the likelihood that the person has abused alcohol or drugs for many years, there are likely to be many problem areas that need to be identified and addressed in the person's recovery. Fourth, if the client is to set goals and direct treatment, he or she needs to be aware of existing strengths. Part of the assessment process involves identifying these strengths. Some clients who have been referred to COPA are in very bad circumstances, and strengths may appear minor. For example, for clients who are very poor, very isolated, and very ill, strengths that can be used in the treatment process might be as mundane as having a relationship with a pet (usually a cat), keeping a tidy house, or even expressing an interest in certain TV programs. Fifth, the philosophy of the COPA program is that all life areas are interrelated. This means that, on the one hand, any reduction in alcohol use may be short-term, if the triggers for use (e.g., loneliness, physical pain) have not been addressed. And, conversely, if a person makes positive changes in other life areas, the substance use may diminish or stop altogether, without any particular focus on it. Finally, attention to all life areas provides the opportunity to engage the client in treatment. Once the person is in treatment, it becomes possible to focus on substance-using behavior directly, if this is needed.

Preparing a Treatment Plan

The COPA counselor helps to identify needs and strengths, but the client must be in control of setting treatment goals. This is especially important at the beginning of treatment. The counselor may have goals for the client, but these can be addressed only when they become the client's goals as well. An example can illustrate the divergence and convergence of client and counselor goals: It has happened that a client has been referred to COPA because he or she is being evicted due to problem behavior while drinking. The client's goal is stable housing and he or she may deny the role of alcohol use in the eviction. The counselor's goal is to reduce the drinking that led to the eviction, so that the problem does not recur. The treatment plan, however, will focus on immediate housing. The goal of reducing drinking can be addressed only when the client is willing.

While treatment goals are individualized for each client, there are certain general goals that tend to apply to most clients:

- stop or reduce alcohol consumption
- receive appropriate medical care
- follow prescribed medication routine
- develop adequate nutrition
- maintain ability to conduct activities of daily living (e.g., care of self and home, shopping, banking, etc.)
- develop/improve marital/family relationships where applicable
- develop/improve non-alcohol-related social and leisure skills and activities
- remain in one's own home or general community noninstitutionalized setting

Finally, the treatment plan often involves accessing other agencies or services, such as a family physician, Meals-on-Wheels, a seniors' center and so on. The role of other agencies in the COPA treatment process will be discussed in greater detail under treatment.

Crisis Intervention

A crisis can be the cause of referral to COPA, as well as the opportunity to engage the client in treatment. Identifying and evaluating urgent or crisis situations is a priority of assessment.

Treatment

The COPA counselors have a generalist, primary care, case management role that includes a wide range of activities. For example, during the time period when data were collected at COPA for the present study, the range of activities by COPA counselors included counseling, support, and education of the client; leading client support groups; counseling of family members of the client; protecting the client from family members; taking the client to a hospital emergency department; advocating for the client with family or agencies; helping the client find a new home; interactions with the client's physician regarding inappropriate prescriptions; arranging psychiatric assessments and case consultations; arranging for a client's apartment to be cleaned after the client died; and feeding a client's cats while the client was in the hospital. The typical contact with a client, however, tends to involve general support and monitoring. Contacts with other agencies are usually for purposes of linking the client to needed services or coordinating the client's care.

A recent study of the case management process at COPA (Graham, Birchmore Timney, & White-Campbell, 1990) found that about 46 percent of contacts were with the client only, 8 percent with a family member, 37 percent with another agency about the client, and the remainder with client and family, client and agency, family and agency; or client, family, and agency. Thus, these results indicate that treatment at COPA involves substantial indirect service to the client (contact with family and other agencies) as well as direct service.

Direct Service to the Client

In order to monitor treatment at COPA, for the present reports, fourteen general categories of services to the client were defined:

- advice (suggestions to the client of ways of coping, courses of action)
- problem solving (helping the client to determine the best course of action)
- goal setting (making specific plans regarding courses of action, activities)
- practical help (helping the client with some activity, e.g., shopping)
- listening (listening to the client)
- empathy (listening to the client and indicating sympathy, empathy, or understanding)
- reinforcement (encouraging the client to *continue* positive behaviors/attitudes)
- encouragement (encouraging the client to *initiate* positive behaviors/attitudes)
- education (providing the client with information, or teaching the client something)

- explanation (clearing up confusion, misunderstandings, or lack of understanding on the part of the client)
- confrontation (making associations between the client's actions and particular undesirable consequences)
- monitoring (obtaining limited information from the client on a regular basis)
- seeking information (probing the client for detailed information on a one-time basis)
- seeking clarification (trying to help the client clarify or define issues)
- other

Some actions are much more frequent than others. For example, listening, empathy, encouragement, and monitoring occur at nearly every contact. On the other hand, practical help, education/explanation, seeking clarification, and goal setting occur least frequently. The type of action taken by the counselor also varies according to the life area being addressed. For example, advice and problem solving are more likely to occur around economic and accommodation issues. Reinforcement and confrontation are more likely to occur regarding alcohol use than in other life areas. Education and practical help are used most frequently regarding drug use.

The following is a brief description of approaches to addressing particular life areas with clients (for more detail, see Saunders et al., 1992).

Alcohol use: Start where the client is (e.g., accept initial denial); identify for the client links between alcohol use and problems in other life areas; reinforce progress made by the client.

Prescription drug use: Make a comprehensive assessment of the client's drug use; ensure that drugs are being used as prescribed (introduce aids such as pill organizers, if needed); identify client-initiated drug abuse, especially of psychoactive medications (including obtaining drugs from more than one doctor); contact prescribing physician if prescribed drugs are causing major problems for the client.

Activities of daily living: Identify limitations to the client's ability to function independently; help client find practical solutions, perhaps with consultation of an occupational therapist; use community support services, as needed.

Medical/dental: Help client establish regular medical and dental care; accompany client to appointments initially, if necessary.

Nutrition: Identify and address problems underlying poor nutrition (e.g., lack of knowledge, inability to shop, depression, poor health); enlist agencies (Meals-on-Wheels), friends, or family to provide some meals for client, if needed.

Marital/family: If the client is married, involvement of the spouse may be needed; it may be necessary to address the spouse's heavy drinking; counseling may need to be provided to family members as well as the client.

Housing: Actions taken by the counselor to resolve housing problems may include advocating for the client, helping the client search for affordable housing, confrontation with the client regarding the role of alcohol use in chronic housing problems, and helping the client find temporary and/or sheltered housing during a crisis.

Finances: Most often, action in this area involves helping the client to obtain all income for which he or she is eligible and helping the client cope with a very low income; the counselor may also have to take action (sometimes legal action) because of income problems due to the client being taken advantage of by family or friends.

Socializing skills and use of leisure time: Identify the client's interests and facilitate pursuit of these interests; enlist a volunteer to provide social support to the client, if possible; if the client has been isolated and is very anxious about new social contacts (at a senior's center, for example), ensure that the client is accompanied (by the counselor, a volunteer, or another client) on initial outings.

Direct Service to the Family

Families may obtain advice and counseling from COPA, even when the older substance abuser is not a client of COPA. In addition, family support and counseling is provided to support the client's treatment, where appropriate. The COPA counselor may help the client reestablish contact with long-lost family members. And, finally, in some circumstances, the COPA counselor will take actions to protect the client from abuse by family members.

*Indirect Service to the Client Through Contact
with Other Agencies–Advocacy and Coordination*

Most communities in North America have set up some level of support services for the older person and others. These include homemaker services, meal services, subsidized housing, and a variety of other services. In addition, the older person is likely to need medical and dental care and sometimes social services. The older alcohol or drug abuser is likely to have problems in a number of life areas where use of existing services would be helpful. In some instances, prior to referral to COPA, clients have been refused services because of their drinking. Treatment at COPA involves activating community supports to help the client resolve existing problems (e.g., medical services for health problems) and to ensure that the client is able to maintain well-being over the long-term (e.g., nutritional support from Meals-on-Wheels). The COPA Program regularly uses over 50 types of services, including medical, dental, financial, housekeeping, and social services, as well as lawyers, public trustees, seniors' centers and resources, occupational therapists, and so on.

The study of case management done at COPA (Graham, Birchmore Timney, & White-Campbell, 1990) found that about 27 percent of agency contacts involved advocacy (obtaining a service for the client, obtaining information or support for the client); 65 percent of contacts involved coordination (case discussion with another agency to develop treatment plan or coordinate treatment, obtaining information from an agency about the client, or keeping another agency (e.g., the referring agent) informed about the client's treatment process); and 7 percent involved both advocacy and coordination. The types of agencies most often involved in the case management process were non-hospital medical programs (e.g., GP, visiting nurse), general or psychiatric hospitals, non-medical counseling programs (e.g., family counselling, social services, occupational therapist), community support services (e.g., homemaker, Meals-on-Wheels, housing worker), and other addictions services (e.g., detox, residential addictions programs).

In summary, other programs play an important role in the COPA treatment approach. They are used to help the client resolve immediate problems, and to provide ongoing support to the client to help maintain gains once treatment at COPA is complete.

Maintaining Gains Made in Treatment/Aftercare

Although there is no predetermined duration of treatment, the more intensive phase of treatment at COPA typically involves weekly contacts with the client to address immediate goals. Once substantial gains have been made and the client's circumstances are stable, frequency of contact typically diminishes to biweekly contacts, and ultimately to occasional phone calls. These contacts serve to let the client know that help is available if needed. Occasionally, clients may move back and forth between active treatment and maintenance several times before achieving stable improvement. Even for clients who do not make substantial progress during active treatment, follow-up contacts are made to provide support and to ensure that help is available for those clients who later become willing to make changes.

Chapter 3

A Typology of COPA Clients

Part of the evaluation of the COPA program included a series of case studies of clients who were experiencing alcohol problems. These were used to formulate a tentative typology of older alcohol abusers. This typology is presented at this stage of the book to orient the reader to the kinds of clients who received services from COPA and to provide a general overview of the variability of the treatment process.[1]

THE NEED FOR A TYPOLOGY OF OLDER PERSONS WHO HAVE ALCOHOL PROBLEMS

One approach to trying to understand the nature of alcohol problems among older people is to try to identify particular types within this target group. Babor and Dolinsky (1988) argued that "to the extent that alcoholic types are readily identifiable, scientifically valid, and clinically meaningful, they can be extremely useful for the purpose of diagnosis and treatment" (p. 260).

Development of a practical typology describing older adults who have alcohol problems seems to be especially important, since this group includes a wide variety of people and problems. It may be that one treatment approach will not be suitable for all individuals within this population, but that successful treatment will be based on identifying subsets of older alcohol abusers who have similarities along dimensions that are relevant to treatment (e.g., nature of problems, etiology of problems, etc.).

---

1. A version of this chapter was published in *Alcoholism Treatment Quarterly,* 9(3/4), 1992 (K. Graham, A. Zeidman, M. C. Flower, S. J. Saunders, and M. White-Campbell.)

In a 1983 paper, Meyer, Babor, and Mirkin reviewed the literature on typologies of alcoholics. They suggested that typologies have been generated using three major methods:

1. intuitive (e.g., Jellinek's typology of alpha, beta, gamma, delta, and epsilon alcoholics; Jellinek, 1960);
2. *a priori* groupings using specific variables to categorize alcoholics on one or two dimensions (e.g., essential-reactive, primary-secondary, male-female); and
3. *a posteriori* correlational approaches using statistical procedures to group alcoholics on a large number of variables (e.g., the three types identified in analyses by Morey, Skinner, and Blashfield, 1984: Type A–early stage problem drinkers; Type B–affiliative, moderate alcohol dependence; and Type C–schizoid, severe alcohol dependence).

Each method has its strengths and weaknesses. The intuitive procedure often seems to capture prevailing beliefs about a phenomenon, but it is not objective and is not based on clear criteria for classification. The *a priori* empirical approach allows objective classification based on theory, but is only suitable for categorizing on one or two dimensions. The *a posteriori* empirical approach is objective but atheoretical, and the types identified using multivariate analyses are often not replicable, because the emergent factors depend strongly on the particular variables and samples in the original analyses.

In general, no typology of alcoholics has been adopted universally (see review by Babor & Dolinsky, 1988). However, with regard to the elderly, the two types proposed by Rosin and Glatt (1971) have been accepted by many in the field. Their two-group typology is based on time of onset: primary causes or early onset (i.e., the chronic excessive drinker), and secondary causes associated with late onset (i.e., the reactive drinker responding to stresses of aging). Recent variations on this typology have been proposed. For example, Gomberg (1982) cited an unpublished report by Carruth and others who suggested a third category, namely, the intermittent problem drinker.

Others have made further distinctions within late-onset drinkers. For example, Giordano and Beckham (1985) identified four patterns among older people who had been classified as late-onset alcohol abusers: (1) the crisis drinker (long history of drinking in response to interpersonal problems), (2) the progressive drinker (moderate drinker who begins to drink heavily in later years), (3) the switched drinker (switching from low alcohol beverages to higher alcohol beverages in later life), and (4) the newcomer (abstainer or very light drinker who takes up drinking in later years) (pp. 68-69). Hubbard, Santos, and Santos, (1979) identified an additional late-onset group who were not technically heavy drinkers, but who experienced problems related to interactions of alcohol with medications.

Although the late-onset/early-onset dichotomy has had some conceptual usefulness, it is also an ambiguous term, particularly with regard to the appropriate age cutoff for delimiting early or late onset. For example, some research has defined "late" onset as beginning as early as age 40 (Atkinson et al., 1985). If, as in this case, "late" onset really means beginning in middle age, this contradicts the usual interpretation (first made by Rosin and Glatt, 1971) of late onset being a phenomenon that occurs as a reaction to particular *stresses of old age* such as retirement or bereavement.

As part of the COPA evaluation, 36 case studies were conducted. The cases were restricted to the first 36 clients who entered the program after a set date and who met the following criteria: enough information was available on the client to develop a comprehensive description (i.e., cases were excluded if the person was seen only briefly, or if no reliable information about his or her substance use could be obtained); and the main problem substance for the client was alcohol. Case descriptions were developed around three major themes: (1) the factors that led to or were associated with substance abuse, (2) the nature of substance abuse and current consequences for the person, and (3) the treatment implications of various abuse patterns. A student (Zeidman) who had served as a clinical intern with the program compiled the case descriptions from case notes, evaluation data, interviews with the case worker, and follow-up interviews (by phone or in person) with each client.

GENERATING PROFILES OR "TYPES" BASED ON CASE STUDIES

An intuitive approach was used to develop a typology of older persons who have alcohol problems. In part, this approach was chosen because of the qualitative nature of the case studies. First, the case study method does not lend itself to statistical "fishing" for types, as characterized by the *a posteriori* method of typing. On the other hand, while it would be possible to use the *a priori* method to create prototypes from case study data according to predetermined dimensions, the *a priori* method does not capitalize on the richness of information available in the case studies.

Although the intuitive method has been criticized because of its subjective nature, subjectivity is present in all methods of classifying. The *a priori* and *a posteriori* methods may be objective in the actual measurement and classification process; nevertheless, subjectivity is involved in the *selection of variables* on which to classify. The intuitive method does not require the same degree of selectivity of variables (as is required by the empirical methods), but it can be affected by personal biases. Therefore, although this study employed an intuitive classification approach, procedures were used to provide some validation of the typology that was generated.

Independently, three of the investigators (two clinicians, one researcher) studied the case histories looking for cases that seemed to be similar, and created groups of similar cases or types. These groups were then examined to identify the defining features of each group. At this point, the three investigators met and discussed their different groupings and developed an initial typology. This typology was tested among other collaborators on the project and revised. The revised topology was then sent to "experts" in the field, that is, professionals who had published in the area of alcohol and the elderly (n = 5), persons working in the general area of gerontology (n = 7), and colleagues working in the general area of alcohol research (n = 8). (For a more detailed description of the process used to validate the typology, see Graham et al., 1989).

The typology developed by the investigators consisted of four "types," depending on what appeared to be the primary factors contributing to the maintenance of alcohol abuse. These types were: (1) chronic alcohol abuser (abusive drinking primarily maintained by a life of habitual consumption and a lack of alternative activities); (2) reactive problem drinker (alcohol abuse developed and maintained in response to a loss, such as ill health or death of a spouse, the person's own poor health and approaching death, or retirement);

(3) problem drinkers whose drinking seemed to be interrelated with psychiatric or cognitive problems; and (4) problem or heavy drinkers whose drinking seemed to be part of a relationship with a heavy-drinking, abusive spouse/partner. The remainder of this chapter focuses on the first three types, as the fourth type (drinking with an abusive spouse) was infrequent among the cases studied.

Although a category was assigned to all 36 cases studied, only 24 were selected to be submitted to external raters. The sample was reduced for the following reasons: to reduce the number of cases to be rated (the largest grouping was the chronic alcohol abusers, and six in this category were dropped), to omit cases which the investigators felt could not easily be classified as one major type (four cases), and leaving out the two cases identified as primarily the fourth type. The sample submitted to expert raters consisted of ten cases identified by the investigators as chronic alcohol abusers, five reactive drinkers, and nine whose alcohol problems seemed to be related to psychiatric or cognitive problems. Of the ten chronic drinkers, all were consistently identified by raters as being this type (i.e., rated in this category by 70 percent or more of the raters). Of the five reactive drinkers, three were rated in this category by all raters, and one by all but one. Ratings of those assigned to the third category (psychiatric or cognitive problems contributing to drinking), however, were not as consistent. Of the nine cases selected by the investigators, only three were rated consistently as this category (i.e., by 70 percent or more of the raters).

The following sections describe each of these types in greater detail, and provide brief case descriptions of those consistently assigned to each category by both the project collaborators and the outside raters. The treatment implications of each typology are described, including an interpretation of the meaning of the inconsistency in ratings for the third category (psychiatric or cognitive problems contributing to drinking).

THE CHRONIC DRINKER

What seemed to define the chronic drinker among older people was the hold on the person of habitual drinking. Whatever life events had first precipitated heavy or problem drinking, the main factor in the person's current drinking appeared to be habit. Depression, poor health, and escape drinking were sometimes triggers; yet the person's drinking did not appear to be primarily reactive. Most did not deny abusing alcohol. Almost half had received treatment previously, nearly all had made previous attempts to reduce drinking, and some had even achieved several years of abstinence. Although some of the chronic drinkers had a stable employment history, most had little money, and many had endured years of skid row living. Even among those with stable employment, all had retired before age 65. Nearly all had experienced substantial losses over the course of their lives, many had chronic health problems, and few had supports outside of the social service system. All the drinkers defined in this category were males, with ages varying from 51 to 72 (average age 61). The following provides brief descriptions of the ten clients classified as chronic drinkers:

Case 1. The client, a 72-year-old male, had a long history of alcohol abuse. Mostly, his drinking was solitary, occasionally social. He told the worker that he drank to relieve pain and depression. The client drank fairly steadily, consuming one-half of a bottle of sherry (four standard drinks)[2] on a moderate day, and three or four bottles or more of stomach bitters (six or more standard drinks) on heavy drinking days. He had some brief periods of abstinence (e.g., when hospitalized for physical health problems). He reported suffering some withdrawal symptoms (shaking, general weakness). The client had severe gastrointestinal problems (aggravated by his drinking), unstable and poor living conditions, no contact with family, poor care of self and living quarters, no friends other than casual drinking companions, poor nutrition, and low motivation.

Case 2. The client was a 60-year-old man who had a long history of alcohol abuse. He attributed some of his heavy drinking to relief of painful memories of when he was a prisoner during World War II. The client's health had deteriorated severely as a result of his prolonged heavy alcohol consumption (liver problems, seizures). He had lost his job a few months before due to his drinking on the

---

2. A standard drink was defined as 12 oz. of 5% beer, 5 oz. of table wine (about 12% alcohol), 3 oz. of fortified wine or sherry (about 18% alcohol), and 1 1/2 oz. of hard liquor (about 40% alcohol).

job. Possibly partly due to his drinking, he was separated from his wife and had poor relationships with his children. At admission, he was lonely and depressed and had no social or leisure activities.

Case 3. This 56-year-old man was referred to COPA by his daughter-in-law, who was concerned about him because he had been on a three-week binge with nothing to eat. The client had a long history of alcohol abuse that included periods of abstinence for up to six months. He had developed a serious drinking problem while working, during which time he associated with heavy drinkers both on and off the job. After taking early retirement at age 57, his drinking increased, especially in terms of binges. At the time of his referral, drinking had become the primary activity in his life. He had liquor delivered to the house, where he drank alone. On a typical binge, he would drink one to two bottles of sherry a day for one to three weeks. During binges, he did not eat and was totally inactive, neglecting his own self-care. His overall lifestyle was lonely and isolated, and he reported that he frequently felt depressed. He had several physical problems resulting from prolonged alcohol abuse, such as hepatitis, peripheral neuropathy, and weight loss. He had also incurred financial problems related to his drinking.

Case 4. The client was a 62-year-old male with a long history of alcohol abuse. He was married with no children. At the time of referral, the client was drinking heavily at home, alone, usually in bed. He seemed to be severely depressed, was very inactive, and slept with a butcher knife under his pillow. He had lost his job three years previously because of his alcohol problem and his subsequent lack of activity seemed to increase his drinking even more. Two years later, his wife had suffered a stroke, and this may have been an additional factor in his depression and drinking. The client had physical health problems, including poor mobility. The client appeared to have no friends and few leisure activities, and his job loss had resulted in financial losses (he had lost his house, car, and savings). At referral, the client was drinking 72 beers per week (consuming 48 of these on the weekend). He slept poorly, had poor appetite, and had experienced withdrawal symptoms including general weakness, hallucinations, and convulsions. His drinking (and related job and financial losses) strained his marriage, and his wife frequently threatened to leave (although she also sometimes supplied his alcohol). The client acknowledged his drinking problem and was particularly aware of the effects of his drinking on his housing and finances.

Case 5. This 63-year-old man had a long history of heavy drinking, both socially and at work. On several occasions, he had been jailed for impaired driving. He also reported a family history of alcoholism. In recent years, his drinking had become more solitary. He drank alone in his apartment, no longer worked, had no social contacts or satisfying leisure pursuits, and had poor health that seemed to limit his activities. He apparently drank in response to loneliness, depression, and boredom. He had been abstinent for several periods in the past (for up to two years). When drinking, he typically reported consuming two to three drinks per day; but, based on his appearance, mood, and visible empties, the worker felt that he was underreporting his alcohol consumption. While drinking, he was mostly inactive, and he neglected self-care and care of his apartment (the rotting food, roaches, maggots, and garbage prompted complaints from his landlord). He neglected nutrition and would often leave meals from Meals-on-Wheels untouched. He had a number of physical health problems (hiatus hernia with esophageal strictures, seizure disorder, chest pains) and was reluctant to seek medical help (especially when drinking). He did not take his medications other than analgesics (which the worker thought he might have been abusing).

Case 6. The client was a 51-year-old man with a long history of alcohol abuse. The client reported that his father, brother, and sister had been alcoholics; that when he was married, his wife also drank heavily; and that over the years his friends and co-workers had been heavy drinkers. He also reported that it was difficult to abstain when he was depressed or discouraged. The client had been admitted to the detox on numerous occasions, and had attended an addictions treatment program five years previously. Following this, he was abstinent for two years, but had gradually resumed heavy drinking. Six months before his referral to COPA, he had suffered a stroke. The stroke seemed to act as a catalyst for his seeking treatment for his alcohol problem. At the time he entered treatment at COPA, he was still in the hospital and had been abstinent for six months. Prior to this, he had been unemployed, in poor health, and lacked appropriate housing. He reported having experienced the following as a consequence of his drinking: had black-outs; was physically abusive (his wife had left him and his children were taken from him); had health problems, including liver damage; had employment problems; and his social/leisure time was dominated by alcohol use.

Case 7. The client was a 65-year-old male with a long history of problem drinking. The client had begun using alcohol in social interactions with his wife, their friends, or at the local pub approximately 30 to 40 years ago. The client seemed to have also used alcohol as a way of creating an emotional escape from a stressful marriage. In addition, the client seemed to be powerfully affected by the deaths of his parents, and the worker noted that this grief was often a trigger to increased drinking, particularly on any date connected with his parents (birthdates, anniversaries, etc.). The client reported a steady intake of two drinks per day (although reports from his wife indicated that his consumption was often much higher). He was reported to become verbally abusive when drunk, especially toward his wife. Although the client was able to follow a daily routine of shopping, cooking, and cleaning, his alcohol abuse resulted in social isolation and a lack of meaningful leisure activities. More recently, the client had increased the amount of drinking he was doing at home, thus aggravating his existing marital conflicts. On one occasion, the client had been taken to a detox center for several days, at which point he was referred to COPA (due primarily to his wife's concern).

Case 8. The client was a 52-year-old male with a 35-year history of problem drinking. He had developed a pattern of heavy social drinking with his wife and with friends. Ten years prior to entering the COPA program, he had attended an inpatient alcohol treatment program, following which he was abstinent for six or seven months. He had also attended AA. Since that time, he had developed chronic health problems, had separated from his wife, and had continued to drink heavily (four to five beers on weekdays, 24 on weekends). Currently, his drinking seemed to be in response to depression, boredom, and physical ailments. He was isolated, inactive, and preoccupied with his illness. When drinking, the client exhibited poor self-care, confusion, slowness, and increased depression (some of these symptoms may have been caused by mixing alcohol and benzodiazepines). He had numerous physical health problems (narcotic bowel, ileostomy, colostomy, abdominal hernia, pancreatitis, respiratory problems, poor appetite, general weakness, insomnia), and the medical report suggested that abstinence from alcohol would be necessary for his health to improve. However, at the same time, worry over his health seemed to elicit heavy drinking. His son (with whom he lived) was supportive of him, but his drinking appeared to have alienated other members of his family.

Case 9. The client was a 63-year-old man with a 40-year history of heavy drinking and drinking-related problems. His drinking had led him to break with his family many years before, and he seemed to have led mostly a skid row lifestyle. He mentioned his long-lost daughter frequently during treatment. At the time of referral to COPA, the client had been drinking heavily for three months after a four-and-a-half-year period of abstinence. He considered himself to be a chronic alcoholic. He was currently sharing an apartment with his girlfriend and another man (also a very heavy drinker). He had set up the apartment so that he could spend most of the day in bed watching TV and drinking beer (later he switched to two bottles of wine per day). According to the client's girlfriend, he was outgoing, energetic, and active when abstinent. When drinking, he became apathetic and let his health suffer by not exercising or taking his medications. He also had experienced the "shakes and D.T.'s." He suffered from heart problems and weakness in his legs, and was hospitalized for these conditions when he had been in treatment for six weeks. He also suffered from depression, and received medication for this while in the program.

Case 10. At referral, this 64-year-old man was spending all his time in his rented room, eating very little, and in deteriorating physical health. He was profoundly depressed, isolated, and inactive. Because of his poor health and lack of mobility, he was not drinking, but according to the referring agent (a community nurse), he had a long history of alcohol abuse (possibly skid row alcoholic life-style).

Treatment and Outcome

In general, treatment with this group focused on reducing drinking, developing other social and leisure activities, helping the person to obtain appropriate health care, resolving economic and housing problems, and providing emotional support and encouragement. Of the ten cases described, three died during treatment or soon after. Of the seven remaining, six showed fairly good outcomes, with three reporting stable abstinence (one with one bout of abusing tranquilizers during the follow-up period), and three reporting reduced drinking from pretreatment levels (with stable functioning in other life areas).

OLDER PERSONS WHOSE PROBLEM DRINKING WAS IN RESPONSE TO GRIEF

These clients demonstrated relatively recent onset of problem drinking in response to one or more of the following: the death or poor health of a spouse, concern about their own poor health and approaching death, or challenges in lifestyle due to retirement. Clients reported that prior to the events precipitating heavy or problem drinking, their drinking was light, "social," or nonproblematic. In support of the clients' reports that previous drinking had been nonproblematic, clients tended to have stable housing and usually a stable job history. They also tended to be more likely to have social supports than the chronic drinkers. It was not usually possible, however, to confirm non-heavy or nonproblematic alcohol consumption prior to the period when problem drinking was identified. In addition, in some cases, the precipitating event had occurred some years previously, resulting in some clients having problems similar to chronic drinkers, such as loss of social supports and low social stability. Of the four in this group, three were men and one was a woman. Ages of the four cases in this group were 57, 68, 80, and 83 (average age of 72). Four cases consistently rated as this type are described below:

Case 11. This 57-year-old male felt that his drinking had become problematic five years previously, following his retirement and the death of his wife. He reported that he drank to cope with depression, isolation, and stress. Recently, he had developed alcohol-induced neuropathy and myopathy which reduced his mobility and limited his activities. His main social contacts were friends who came to his apartment to drink with him. He usually drank three to ten drinks per day. The major negative effects of his drinking were the alcohol-related physical health problems he experienced. He also reported unsatisfactory relationships with his children and lost contact with his church, possibly because of his drinking. The client was bothered by the effect of his drinking on his self-esteem and emotional health (at times when drinking heavily he became weepy and expressed guilt).

Case 12. The client was a 68-year-old male who began drinking heavily following the lengthy illness (eight years) and death of his wife six years before. Following his wife's death, he retired from a job that he had liked, sold his home, furnishings, and pets, dropped all his friends, and moved to Toronto. He became very depressed, and began drinking heavily to fill time. Also, for the previous year or so, he had been keeping company with a girlfriend who was also a heavy drinker. During treatment, his sister developed cancer, which seemed to further increase his drinking. The client reported that he drank in bars in order to have the company of others. He also reported that he drank when he became depressed even though drinking made his depression worse. In addition, anniversary dates related to his deceased wife often precipitated increased drinking. The client had a binge pattern of drinking (consuming 4-12+ drinks per day), and often at the end of a binge would admit himself to a detox center. After a binge, he would abstain for two to three months and then go on another binge. When he was drinking he became more depressed, apathetic, withdrawn, remorseful, and low in self-esteem. He did not show up for appointments when drinking, ignored care of self and home, and spent a lot of money. During the years of drinking since retirement, he had spent most of his savings and was living in a small, expensive apartment. He had few friends who were not heavy drinkers and no meaningful leisure pursuits.

Case 13. This 80-year-old woman reported that she began drinking heavily (about ten drinks per day) during the past few years in response to her own poor health, her husband's poor health (which made him unable to communicate), to relieve boredom, to sleep better, and to cope with depression and hopelessness. She felt that her consumption had not been problematic prior to the past few years. Her consumption appeared to increase her depression and prevent her from having satisfying social contacts and leisure time.

Case 14. This 83-year-old male had been a social drinker, but when his wife suffered a stroke and was placed in a nursing home, his drinking became heavier and began to cause some problems for him. He was living in his own home and was visited daily by neighbors and family (who also brought him meals). The client had some physical health problems and some memory deficits, but his major problem was the loss of his wife. This caused him to be lonely and depressed, and had led to heavy drinking prior to admission to the hospital (from which he had been referred to COPA).

Treatment and Outcome

Clients identified as this type received emotional support including grief counseling, education about the effects of alcohol on health and other life areas, and help getting their lives back together where substantial deterioration had occurred. Although older than the chronic drinkers, none of these clients died during treatment or follow-up. All demonstrated good outcomes at follow-up, with one reporting abstinence, two reporting occasional light drinking, and one reporting occasional heavy drinking.

OLDER DRINKERS WHOSE COGNITIVE/PSYCHIATRIC PROBLEMS APPEARED TO CONTRIBUTE TO ABUSIVE DRINKING

During the case analyses, the investigators identified a subgroup of clients who did not appear to fit either the pattern of the long-term, chronic alcohol abusers or the recent-onset, reactive problem drinkers. This type seemed to be primarily defined by irrational thinking and a dissociation of self from alcohol problems. Among the clients of this type, it was often difficult to establish the duration of problem drinking, although in some cases long-term alcohol abuse was clearly evident. Other cases appeared to be somewhat similar to the reactive drinker type, in that grief appeared to be a powerful dynamic in precipitating drinking bouts. As perceived by the investigators, however, the primary contributing factor to alcohol abuse was a preexisting psychiatric disorder or ongoing or

intermittent cognitive problems.[3] This type of client was characterized by a lack of understanding about drinking, or about drinking
behavior as something he or she might try to control. They tended
to engage in binge drinking; to exhibit bizarre, unruly, or disoriented behavior while drinking; and to completely neglect care of
self and living quarters while drinking. This type of client was
likely to be already living in a supportive environment (e.g., home
for the aged) or to be managing poorly living in the community.
They were most likely to be referred because of concerns about
their inability to maintain independent living or because of distur-
bances caused when drinking.

Although this was seen as a definite category by investigators, it
tended to be a type that was not consistently categorized by external
raters. Of the nine clients selected for submission to expert raters,
only three received a consistent rating of this type (two by 90
percent of raters and one by 70 percent). The remaining cases
defined by the investigators as this type tended to receive no consistent category from expert raters. This inconsistency likely resulted
because cases defined as this type also usually exhibit either long-
term alcohol abuse, or drink apparently in relation to grief about an
identifiable event. Nevertheless, among the investigators (four of
whom were clinicians), this was seen as a clear clinical type for
whom age of onset was not the critical dimension.

Although the external raters tended not to distinguish this type
from the other two types, the three case examples that were consistently rated as this type are presented here in order to raise the issue
of the role of psychiatric or cognitive problems among elderly alcohol abusers. To our knowledge, nothing has been published on this
topic. Yet, experience at COPA suggested that, cases of this type tend
to be more complex than other cases. In addition, for these cases, it
was often difficult to identify the best strategies for helping the client
reduce alcohol use. The cases presented here may be helpful in
designing research to understand more fully those elderly alcohol
abusers whose drinking seems to be linked more to psychiatric or

---

3. Note: Not all clients who exhibited cognitive impairment were classified as
this category–only those whose cognitive impairment seemed to contribute to their
drinking problems.

cognitive problems than to long-term consumption patterns or reactive drinking. Of the three cases consistently identified as this type, all were female. Among the other six cases identified by the investigators (but not consistently rated), most were female. Perhaps the defining feature of the category–namely, irrational thinking and denial–was a reflection of a generation of women unable to accept not only the label but even the experience of alcohol abuse. This group tended to be younger than the reactive drinkers (average age of 58 for the three consistently rated; average age of 67 for all nine identified by investigators). The three consistently rated cases are described by the following:

Case 15. The client was a 59-year-old woman. She had a long history of housing instability, low income (single mother on welfare), and binge drinking. She was also manic-depressive with poorly controlled symptoms. Her binges seemed to coincide with the extremes of her mood swings. She was in poor health, very isolated, and very inactive. At the time of referral, the client had been recently discharged from the hospital and was still very ill with digestive and bowel problems, possibly related to drinking. Other life areas that seemed to have been negatively affected by her drinking were: her relationship with her daughter; housing; moods; nutrition; and ability to care for herself. When drinking, she sometimes became quite ill, her personal appearance deteriorated, she was unable to comply with her medications regime, and she sometimes became unruly and verbally abusive.

Case 16. This 54-year-old woman was first seen in the hospital where she had been admitted with diagnosis of alcoholic dementia (and was referred to COPA by a social worker there). At this initial visit, she admitted drinking 4 oz. of hard liquor four times daily (ten standard drinks) and reported drinking alcohol from age 12. Her father had been alcoholic and abusive. Although she had living siblings and a son, she did not appear to have significant contacts with them. There was no information concerning the past role of alcohol in her life, but she had a history of psychiatric problems (initial diagnosis of schizophrenia). The client had few social or leisure contacts that did not involve drinking (she had one long-standing friend who was aware of her drinking problem), and was referred because she had problems with independent community living when drinking. The effects of her drinking were evident on her mental health, housing, care of self and living quarters, financial status, and legal status. Although she denied any problems with alcohol, she accepted help from the program because she wanted to return to living independently and not be institutionalized.

Case 17. The client was a 62-year-old woman. She had a history of psychiatric problems (she had been diagnosed as having chronic organic brain syndrome, mood disorders, grandiose ideas, mania, schizophrenia, and syphilis). At admission, she also reported marital problems and showed symptoms of depression. Prior to entering the program, she had been drinking heavily (one bottle of rye whisky per day–18 standard drinks). During this time she did not eat for ten days and was ultimately hospitalized. When drinking, she became violent and abusive. She also neglected to take her medications, resulting in worsening of her psychiatric problems. In addition to chronic organic brain syndrome, she had a number of physical health problems that may have been related to or aggravated by her alcohol consumption, including gastrointestinal bleeding, liver cirrhosis, neuropathy, and angina. The client was aware of her alcohol problems, referring to herself as an alcoholic, but she did not seem to connect her consumption to her health problems, psychiatric problems, or marital problems. Her housing, financial, and legal statuses appeared to be stable. It was reported in the case notes that she had been married eight times, and had two children and several siblings, but the status of her relationships with family members (other than her current spouse) was unknown; there was also little information about her social/leisure activities (although she did go on holidays to Miami and other places).

Treatment and Outcome

If a client was being treated for a psychiatric disorder, often the first priority was to stabilize this treatment (particularly compliance with medications). Other aspects of treatment tended to relate to dealing with the sequelae of the person's problem drinking, such as helping with housing, economic, or legal problems. Treatment for this type of alcohol abuser also included education about the effects of alcohol and alcohol-drug interactions, support and encouragement, and assistance in making lifestyle changes, particularly with regard to social/leisure activities.

Of the three consistently rated, two became abstinent (one after she moved to a rest home), and one reduced her drinking (although she had one major relapse during the follow-up period). For the six others not consistently rated, outcomes were not as good. Three deteriorated substantially in cognitive functioning (two were institutionalized, one went to live with her daughter), one died, one became abstinent but continued to have severe psychiatric problems, and one was living in a nursing home, doing well and drinking occasionally.

DISCUSSION

This study confirmed the distinction previously made between chronic and reactive older alcohol abusers. These two groups appeared to have different factors contributing to drinking, with the chronic alcohol abusers' drinking forming part of a long-established alcohol abusing lifestyle, and the reactive drinkers apparently drinking in response to a particular event or events in their lives. Correspondingly, the treatment approaches for the two types were different. While all clients received emotional support and encouragement from the worker, as well as suggestions to reduce drinking, the chronic drinkers tended to need more help with establishing economic and social stability in their lives. On the other hand, grief counseling was usually provided to reactive clients to resolve some of the feelings that were maintaining their drinking. In addition, they often received education about the effects of alcohol to clarify how their drinking appeared to be affecting other aspects of their lives.

In developing the typology, the third type (drinking affected by cognitive/psychiatric problems) was seen as a type worth separating from the chronic and reactive drinkers in that it reflected a person who could not control his or her drinking or drinking behavior–not because of a chronic pattern of drinking or because of reaction to grief, but rather because of cognitive or psychiatric problems and/or an inability to *understand* the process and effects of his or her own drinking. Of the expert raters who submitted comments, some felt that this type defined a useful distinction; others felt that such cases could be considered a subtype of the other two types; and one suggested that this type was simply another version of the chronic heavy drinker. From the perspective of treatment, however, there appeared to be a valid (if somewhat vague) difference in the treatment process of this type of client from the other two types.

In general, treatment focused on grief counseling for the reactive drinkers (possibly with some lifestyle counseling), and lifestyle counseling for the chronic drinkers (possibly with some grief counseling). For those with psychiatric, cognitive, or behavioral problems, the treatment approach was less clear. In at least one case, the psychiatric disorder (manic depression) had to be brought under control in order to make progress with reducing drinking. Others reduced drinking without any special attention paid to concurrent psychiatric or cognitive problems. For others, the cognitive impairment and irrational thinking seemed to prevent successful treatment (e.g., clients who were hostile and irrational in response to suggestions by the worker about reducing substance use).

This typology clarifies the nature of alcohol problems among older persons and the type of treatment that seems most appropriate. Treatment of older alcohol abusers in these case studies generally focused on two main areas (in addition to trying to convince the person to reduce or eliminate alcohol use): (1) reducing the aspects of life that maintained drinking (e.g., a lack of alternative activities, grief, cognitive or psychiatric impairment), and (2) helping the clients in other life areas where other problems had developed (as a result of drinking, aging, or both). Although treatment needs to be designed to suit individual needs, a broad typology, such as the one proposed here, can help the clinician target more readily the factors within the client's life that are helping to maintain the person's alcohol abuse. Developing desirable alternatives for the chronic drinker, helping the reactive drinker to resolve some of the grief feelings, and stabilizing the psychiatric problems of the problem drinker are likely to be fundamental aspects of successful treatment.

Chapter 4

Evaluation Research at COPA: Goals, Methods, and Problems

The COPA program was an innovative and unorthodox approach to addictions treatment for a population about which very little was known. Therefore a major component of the program was evaluation research. Evaluation research at COPA was designed to be exploratory and to provide an in-depth description of the nature of problems and the process of recovery among older substance abusers.

THE GOALS OF RESEARCH AT COPA

The main goals of the evaluation research at COPA were:

- *To develop valid measures of client status in alcohol and drug use and other life areas, and to monitor client changes during treatment at COPA.* Valid measures of client status were needed, first to assess client change from entry to discharge from the program, and second, to develop a better description of the population of older adult substance abusers.
- *To identify factors associated with recovery in this population.* For this objective, client characteristics and other factors would be analyzed as predictors of client change during treatment.

METHODS

The design of the research was descriptive, involving three types of data:

1. intake and assessment data concerning the client's background and current status, collected at entry into the program
2. client contact data collected after every contact with the client, including data concerning the events that occurred at the contact and the client's current status at the time of the contact
3. discharge data, including a brief description of the client's disposition at discharge.

Later in the project, a fourth type of data was incorporated, which consisted of:

4. 36 case studies (using the evaluation data as well as descriptive case notes and follow-up interviews with the clients).

The assessment and discharge data were collected primarily for clinical or program purposes, and secondarily for research purposes. The client contact data were intended to form the major database for addressing research questions. There were several factors involved in the decision to focus on client contact data as the major source of information. The first factor was the issue of the burden of research on the client. It was resolved at the outset that the clinical needs of the clients would always take precedence over the research needs. This meant that clients could not be subjected to lengthy questioning on issues that the client was uncomfortable or uninterested in addressing. Thus, the usual method in addictions treatment research of using lengthy assessment questionnaires could not be employed. The second issue that led to placing secondary importance on assessment or discharge data was the question of reliability and validity. The program's explicit mandate to help people *whether or not they were willing to acknowledge substance-related problems* suggested *a priori* that the information provided by the clients when first entering the program would be highly suspect. The contact data, on the other hand, provided a standardized method of collecting information that could be averaged (thus improving reliability) and could incorporate the counselor's perceptions and knowledge about the client (thus improving validity by not being based exclusively on self-report). Nevertheless, while primary weight was to be given to the monitoring data (i.e., client contact data) in estimating outcomes, all sources of data were used to address the research objectives.

Assessment Data

The assessment form was completed by the counselor after a maximum of four contacts with client. Information was obtained through informal interviews with the client, during which the counselor made notes. Later these notes were used as memory aids when the counselor completed the actual assessment form at the office.

The assessment form was developed to ensure a comprehensive clinical assessment and to collect background data for research purposes. The form consisted of 48 pages of questions regarding the client's background and status in a variety of life areas (from medical history to frequency of social contacts).[1] The assessment form depended primarily on self-report by the client, but also included items for recording reports from other sources regarding the client's substance use and substance-related problems. The items included in the assessment form were usually closed-ended, using either dichotomous categories or a rating scale (scales varied from 3 points to 7 points). Not all the data collected on the assessment form were useful for research purposes.

Monitoring (Client Contact) Data

The client contact forms were completed following every contact with the client (face-to-face, telephone, written, etc.). Ideally, these forms were to be completed immediately following the contact with the client, although in practice this did not always occur. Thus, while the data collected using the contact forms were generally reliable and consistent, some additional error variability was introduced by the delay in reporting.

Because the contact form was the main source of research data for monitoring client progress and program interventions, a great deal of effort was expended to develop a form that was valid, included information that was useful to the counselor, and included the kinds of items that could be completed in a standardized format across clients. The form was developed in an iterative fashion, beginning

---

1. Because of the length of the assessment form, it is not included in this book. The assessment form was published previously as an ARF Internal Document (Saunders et al., 1985). See Appendix B for current assessment form.

with structured case notes and moving increasingly from a qualitative to a quantitative format (this process was described in Graham & Timney, 1985).

The final form (see Appendix A) included a summary sheet describing the client's general status in all life areas. It also included forms for each life area that were completed following contacts with a client at which particular areas were identified as problematic (these additional forms are not included in Appendix A). Because the summary sheets contained the most complete data, they formed the basis for most of the data analysis regarding client outcomes.

In the development of the form, two small inter-rater reliability studies were done using an observer at client contacts. The study of inter-rater reliability of the final forms (Graham, 1987) found generally good agreement on most client status variables, with highest agreement (coefficients of agreement of 0.70 or greater) on the more observable life areas such as emotional health, personal hygiene, accommodation problems, economic problems, relationship with spouse, and recent alcohol use. Other areas, such as physical health and leisure problems, showed lower agreement. The size of the scales also affected their reliability, with longer scales being generally more reliable. Scales varied from 3-point scales (e.g., leisure) to 100-point scales (e.g., physical, emotional, and mental health). The COPA counselors preferred shorter scales where each value had a label attached to it. On the other hand, the smaller scales were less useful for research purposes. The findings concerning inter-rater reliability were interpreted as low estimates of the true reliability of reporting, in that inter-rater disagreement could be attributed to a number of factors (such as the worker having more knowledge of the client than the observer had) that were not really reflective of the actual reliability of the scales, as used in the study.

Discharge Data

The discharge form was developed by the clinical staff at COPA for clinical uses and program statistics. It included information concerning the date of the client's last contact with the program, length of stay, reasons for discharge, whether treatment was completed, and other variables relating to client's overall status at termination. Although the form was not intended to measure outcomes for research purposes (outcome was to be measured by monitoring client status using the client contact forms), the discharge form did provide a clinical perspective that was useful for the data analyses.

Case Studies Data

The case studies were funded as a separate project in 1987 (see Graham et al., 1989, for final report of case study research). The case studies used existing data on COPA clients as well as follow-up data obtained either directly from the clients or from someone else who knew the client's follow-up status. A general description of the case studies was provided in Chapter 3.

DESCRIPTION OF TREATMENT CONTACTS DURING THE EVALUATION PERIOD

Monitoring data were collected at 1,717 client contacts involving 113 clients. Analyses of these data, however, were restricted to the 1,114 contacts involving the 56 clients who *began* and *completed* treatment during the data collection period. The following description of the client contact data is based on the 1,114 contacts included in the data analyses.

Contacts with clients occurred in a variety of places: 593 home visits (54 percent), 282 office visits (26 percent), 101 telephone contacts[2] with the client (9 percent); 95 contacts where the worker accompanied the client somewhere, usually to the hospital or doctor's office (9 percent); 17 accidental contacts with clients (e.g., met client on the street) (2 percent); and 19 other types of contacts (2 percent).

The duration of contacts varied from one minute to six hours with an average duration of 44 minutes. Most contacts were classified as "regular" contacts (69 percent of all contacts); other types of contacts included brief information exchange (8 percent), drop-in visit by the client (4 percent), visit to the client while he or she was in the

---

2. This underestimates the number of telephone contacts with clients, as telephone contacts were not always documented.

hospital or in residential treatment (5 percent), crisis visit (3 percent), other specific purpose for visit (3 percent), COPA group (3 percent), accompanying the client somewhere (2 percent), visit to the client by request of family or someone else (2 percent), special occasion visit (e.g., birthday) (1 percent), and other (1 percent). There was someone else present, other than the client and the counselor, at 29 percent of the contacts. Most often this was the spouse (about 12 percent of all contacts); other persons present included other family, friends, landlady, COPA volunteer, COPA observer, nurse, physician, or other agency personnel.

SAMPLE SIZE AND OTHER CHARACTERISTICS OF CLIENTS WHO PARTICIPATED IN THE RESEARCH

There were two main sources of data used in the analyses: assessment data and monitoring data. Assessment data were available on 91 clients, and these data were used in the analyses of factors associated with alcohol and drug problems among older people. Monitoring data were used for only a subset (n = 56) of those assessed.

Monitoring data were used to measure outcomes and were limited to those who began and completed treatment during the data collection period. Because of the unusual approach of COPA (namely, outreach to older persons who were not necessarily willing to admit to having an alcohol or drug problem), cases included in the monitoring data were further restricted to those clients who had "engaged" in treatment, at least minimally. That is, monitoring data were used only for those clients who met at least one of two criteria: (1) seen by the counselor at least five times, or (2) seen less than five times but considered to have received at least some treatment (more than just intake). The decision to exclude cases seen less than five times was made for two reasons. First, the data analyses were based on changes observed during treatment, and at least five ratings for each client were considered necessary for analyses. Second, and probably more importantly, many of those seen only one or two times could not be considered to have entered treatment. For example, a person might be referred to COPA and see a counselor several times before making it clear to the worker that help was *not* desired. Alternatively, a person might be referred for suspected substance abuse and it may take the counselor several visits to establish that substance abuse was incorrectly identified as a problem. Including such cases in outcome analyses would be inappropriate. Therefore, five visits was set as an arbitrary cutoff (i.e., if a person received at least five visits they were considered to have been "in treatment"). For those who received less than five visits, the worker was asked to specify whether or not they actually seemed to enter treatment (and thus should be retained in the analyses). The number of visits per client for the 56 clients involved in the data analyses of the monitoring variables ranged from two to 95 (including eight cases who received less than five visits), with a mean of 20 visits per client and a median of 13 visits.

Table 1 shows the frequencies of categories of sex, marital status, and general referral source, as well as the mean age at assessment for clients included in the assessment sample and the monitoring sample. Both samples consisted of approximately two-thirds males. There was a fairly even distribution across marital status categories, with married and widowed persons slightly more frequent than other categories. The proportion of those in the separated or divorced categories was much higher than would be expected for this age group on the basis of Canadian Census data (Statistics Canada, 1987), and higher than was found in a recent survey of seniors' apartments in Toronto (Adlaf, Smart, & Jansen, 1989).

The largest proportion of referrals were from visiting nurses and "other" (a catch-all category including social services, seniors centers, banks, taxi drivers, etc.). Self-referrals accounted for only about 5 to 6 percent of clients. The average age of clients was 64 to 65. The program targeted persons who were 55 or older, but persons under 55 were accepted if the program seemed appropriate for the person. The age range of the sample was 46 to 85.

EVALUATION ISSUES

Because of the innovative nature of the program and the implications of the project for future programming for older persons, research was seen to be an important aspect of program development.

TABLE 1. Characteristics of Clients Used in the Two Levels of Data Analysis

	Assessment (n = 91)		Monitoring (n = 56)	
Sex:				
male	55	(65%)	37	(66%)
female	36	(40%)	19	(34%)
Marital status:				
ever single	13	(14%)	11	(20%)
married/cohabiting	26	(29%)	14	(25%)
separated	14	(15%)	10	(18%)
divorced	15	(17%)	9	(16%)
widowed	23	(25%)	12	(21%)
Referral source:				
visiting nurse	32	(36%)	17	(30%)
other medical	18	(20%)	10	(18%)
family/friend	13	(15%)	8	(14%)
self	5	(6%)	3	(5%)
other	21	(24%)	18	(32%)
Average age in years	65		64	

However, there were a number of problems in designing an appropriate evaluation strategy for the COPA project. These included: a lack of valid measures of substance abuse among older persons; the focus of the program on helping clients in a number of life areas (not just their substance use) and the lack of valid measures for monitoring other life areas; the individualized and flexible nature of the treatment where each client received a unique treatment intervention (i.e., no standard interventions and no standard length of involvement with the program); and the unknown impact of the age and past history of the clients on expected outcomes.

Difficulties in Measuring Substance Abuse Among Older Adults

As the research program evolved, it became apparent that measuring alcohol abuse among older adults was an issue that had received little attention, and no existing measures of alcohol abuse that had been developed for the general population had been validated specifically for older people (Graham, 1986). In addition, nearly all existing measures of alcohol abuse relied heavily (or completely) on self-report measures, an approach that was not appropriate for the COPA project, which specifically targeted hard-to-reach older persons who were not prepared to admit to alcohol problems.

As with alcohol abuse, drug abuse among older people had not been well-defined. For older persons (at least for people who are currently in older age groups), drug abuse or drug problems are almost always related to prescription drug use, whereas use of illicit drugs is very rare (Atkinson, 1984; McKim & Mishara, 1987). At present, there are no established norms or valid measures of what constitutes prescription drug abuse among older people. Moreover, the usual goal for drug abusers–of being drug-free or abstinent–may not be possible or even desirable for the older person who has developed prescription drug-related problems. Thus, the immediate problem of the research was how to monitor and assess changes in substance abuse among COPA clients.

Lack of Valid Measures for Monitoring Changes in Other Life Areas Among the Elderly

Saunders' earlier clinical experience suggested that help for substance-abusing elderly persons should be broadly focused, and that improvement in other life areas should be part of the program objectives. In theory, if substance abuse is perceived to be part of a system of behavior, interventions would focus on the most responsive part of the system, but changes across the system would be expected. For example, the socially isolated, depressed older alcohol abuser may drink because of social isolation and depression or, alternatively, may be socially isolated and depressed because of his or her drinking. Regardless of the direction of causality, however, the intervention may achieve success by focusing on any or all of the interrelated problems. For example, reducing the person's social isolation may increase self-esteem, reduce depression, and reduce the extent of alcohol use. On the other hand, reducing drinking might result in the person becoming less depressed and more socially active. One of the guiding principles of the COPA program was that the client should be given help in the areas that she or he designated as priorities, and that this indirect approach would ultimately reduce substance use. Thus, while the focus of the program was on substance abuse, the overall goal was improved quality of life (including but not restricted to reduced substance abuse) and maintaining independent living. It was, therefore, important for the research to include measurement of changes in life areas other than substance use, not only as an alternative indicator of program effectiveness where changes in substance abuse could not be established, but also: (1) to identify the life areas that COPA was not able to affect, and (2) to assess the relationship between changes in substance abuse and changes in other life areas. Although measurement regarding the well-being of older persons has made some progress in recent years (see, for example, the recent monograph by Kozma, Stones, & McNeil, 1991), at the time this project began in 1985, few standard tools were available to be incorporated into the evaluation.

The Individualized and Flexible Nature of Treatment

Every client received unique treatment at COPA. There was no set length of treatment or standard interventions. This variability made it difficult to interpret and generalize results. Some attempts were made to monitor treatment delivery in order to identify the effective aspects of treatment; however, this quantitative approach was unable to identify the critical aspects of treatment. Therefore, the outcome evaluation at COPA provides information about the success of the overall approach but not evaluation of specific interventions with clients. The 36 case studies conducted as part of the evaluation were used to provide some basis for speculation regarding the critical aspects of treatment for particular clients.

Expectations Regarding Outcomes for Elderly Substance Abusers

Certain attributes of older people make program evaluation more difficult than evaluating programs treating younger persons. First, regardless of the efficacy of a program, it can be expected that among older people there will be losses of subjects due to death, institutionalization, cognitive impairment, and so on. Second, some older clients may be unwilling or unable to participate in extensive research interviews (particularly clients, such as those at COPA, who are in the program because of outreach efforts rather than as self-referred voluntary participants). Although the research literature (Miller & Hester, 1980; 1986) provides some basis for estimating normative success rates from conventional addictions treatment programs, no normative rates have been established specifically for older substance abusers. Even more uncertain is the expected success rate of programs such as COPA, which have an unconventional approach to addictions treatment (outreach, tolerance of denial). Ideally, the COPA research would have involved a control group of older persons who did not receive treatment, in order to assess the effectiveness of COPA. However, the use of randomization to a no-treatment control group for a program such as COPA may well be impossible. Most of the information that was obtained to assess the client's progress in treatment was obtained *only by building trust between the counselor and the client and by engaging the client in the treatment process.* Thus, it would be impossible to obtain sufficient accurate data on a no-treatment control group.

THE FOCUS OF THE DATA ANALYSES

The evaluation research at COPA focused on describing:

- the characteristics of older substance abusers
- the changes that clients made while in treatment.

The characteristics of older substance abusers is the focus of the next three chapters. Chapter 5 contains a literature review of factors associated with substance abuse among older people. Chapter 6 describes the characteristics of COPA clients, and Chapter 7 provides a discussion of these characteristics in the context of existing knowledge about the characteristics of older substance abusers.

Subsequent chapters focus on client outcomes. Chapter 8 describes how outcomes were measured. The changes made by the clients (i.e., client outcomes) are described in Chapter 9. Chapter 10 describes the factors associated with recovery, evaluating the role of client characteristics and other factors in the progress made in treatment.

Chapter 5

Literature Review of Factors Related to Drinking Problems Among Older Adults

In the addictions field in general, it is often difficult to identify which factors are causes and which are effects of substance abuse (see review by Graham & Ekdahl, 1986). With older problem drinkers, distinguishing cause from effect can be even more problematic, as it is often impossible to identify which drinking-related factors *preceded* heavy drinking when the drinking pattern has evolved over 40 or 50 years.[1]

Even with "late-onset" alcohol abuse among older people (i.e., alcohol abuse that begins at middle age or later), causal factors are difficult to identify. This is most clearly demonstrated by the fairly large quantity of literature on the role of stresses/losses of aging (bereavement, retirement, loneliness, poor health) in the development of problem drinking. As pointed out by two somewhat recent reviews (Finney & Moos, 1984; Giordano & Beckham, 1985), clinical studies of older persons who have alcohol problems (Droller, 1964; Rosin & Glatt, 1971) have identified stresses of aging as major factors in the development of alcohol problems; however, epidemiological studies have found no relationship between age-related stressful life events and heavy or problem drinking (Barnes, 1982). Based on a model reported by Mackie in 1974 (cited by Finney & Moos 1984), Finney and Moos (1984) proposed that

---

1. The focus of the literature review is on factors related to *drinking* problems, since drug abuse among the elderly has not been well-defined or studied. A few studies cited, however, do include a general category of substance abusers (i.e., older persons abusing either alcohol and/or drugs).

stress as a causal factor in alcohol abuse might be considered an "INUS condition–that is, it is an *i*nsufficient but *n*on-redundant (it provides an independent contribution) component of an *u*nnecessary (other combinations of factors can also produce problem drinking) but *s*ufficient composite condition" (p. 280). To expand on this statement in the present context, stresses of aging:

1. are an insufficient cause of alcohol abuse (i.e., some people experience stresses of aging and do not increase alcohol consumption or problems, or possibly even decrease alcohol consumption);
2. are a nonredundant component in the development of alcohol abuse (i.e., these stresses do play an independent contributing causal role, but only in conjunction with other factors such as previous drinking patterns, available coping strategies, and so on);
3. are an unnecessary condition (i.e., alcohol abuse can develop among older people in the absence of obvious stresses of aging); and
4. when combined with other factors, form a sufficient composite condition.

Some recent findings by Valanis, Yeaworth, & Resing Mullis (1987) on the relationship between bereavement and alcohol consumption support this more complex notion of causality. They found that while there was no overall increase in drinking following the death of a spouse, certain subgroups did increase: men, those who were poorer, and those who were more depressed at three months following the spouse's death.

Although simple causal theories cannot be applied directly to the study of older problem drinkers, it is, nonetheless, important to develop some understanding of the factors *associated* with alcohol abuse among this age group. Successful case identification strategies and successful interventions are most likely to be based on a good understanding of the interrelationships of substance use with other aspects of the person's life.

SUMMARY OF EXISTING LITERATURE

A large number of papers pertaining to alcohol use among older people have been published. These papers, however, vary greatly in quality. In addition, the papers appear in journals from a wide range of disciplines and many are only available in reports of limited circulation. Moreover, many of the most-cited reports consist of a confusing mixture of clinical opinion and original data. In recent years, there have been a number of reviews in this area (Atkinson, Ganzini, & Bernstein, 1992; Giordano & Beckham, 1985; Gomberg, 1982; Finney & Moos, 1984; Mishara & Kastenbaum, 1980; Williams, 1984); therefore, another review will not be attempted here. Instead, a list of factors associated with alcohol abuse among older persons will be generated on the basis of those publications that contain original data on older persons who have alcohol problems. In particular, the focus will be on identifying factors that help to describe and understand the nature (predictors, process, consequences) of alcohol problems among older adults.

There have been two main sources of data on this topic: general population surveys; and reports about older persons treated for addictions problems either in conventional addictions treatment programs, in general psychiatric programs, or in psychogeriatric programs. All sources of information are problematic. First, the general population surveys tend to find very low rates of alcohol problems among older age groups. Thus, although the original sample size may have been large in these surveys, the number of older people who were identified by these surveys as having alcohol problems has usually been very small–too small for conducting subanalyses to determine the factors associated with problem drinking. For example, several large-scale surveys have been done recently; one by Barnes (1982) in upper New York State, another by a group of researchers as part of the NIMH Epidemiologic Catchment Area Project (ECA Project) (Blazer et al., 1984), and a third reported by Warheit and Auth (1984). In the Barnes study, the survey sample size was 1,041; however, of these, only 31 people aged 60 or over were identified as heavy drinkers (drinking 1 oz. or more of absolute alcohol daily). From the ECA Project, Blazer et al. (1984) based their report on a sample of 3,796 persons surveyed in North

Carolina; however, of these, only 21 people aged 60 or over were diagnosed as current alcoholics (117 were identified with a lifetime diagnosis of alcohol abuse and/or dependence, and 49 reported at least one symptom of alcohol abuse or dependence in the prior year). Warheit and Auth's study, done as part of a large multi-site mental health project, included over 4,000 respondents, with 1,820 who were 50 years of age or older. Of the people over 50, only 42 were designated as high risk alcohol users. Thus, although the large-scale surveys can provide the most objective method for identifying characteristics of older persons who have alcohol problems compared to other groups, these surveys are not as useful as they appear to be because the numbers of older people identified as alcohol abusers have been small. In addition, there is some concern that community surveys tend to miss some groups of older persons who have higher rates of alcohol problems because (1) nursing homes, homes for the aged, and hostels are often not included in the sampling; and (2) older persons who have alcohol problems may be more likely to refuse to participate or be unable to participate.

Two surveys were able to identify sufficient numbers of older substance abusers to analyze factors associated with abuse. First, a survey by Rathbone-McCuan et al. (1976) which used several procedures specially designed to identify older persons who had alcohol problems, was more successful than other surveys in describing a number of distinguishing characteristics of older alcohol abusers compared to older people who did not have alcohol problems. Similarly, a recent survey of residents of senior citizen apartments conducted in Toronto, Canada (Adlaf, Smart, & Jansen, 1989) used sensitive measures of substance abuse to identify abusers or potential abusers. Procedures included selection of a sample of 500 apartments, of which 64 percent agreed to participate in a one-hour interview. Adlaf, Smart, and Jansen were unable to estimate the extent to which the 35 percent refusal rate resulted in a selection bias, but it might be argued that the heavier substance abusers would be more likely to refuse to participate and would be underrepresented in the sample. Thus, although their study was better able than some previous studies to compare abusers and nonabusers, even their procedures may well have missed some of the older people who had the most severe problems.

Studies of specific samples of older people who have alcohol problems have also had methodological problems that make interpretation somewhat problematic. These studies tend to be based on two types of samples: (1) clients of traditional treatment programs who happen to be elderly (Schuckit, Morrissey, & O'Leary, 1978), and (2) older alcohol abusers identified in populations of psychiatric, psychogeriatric, or social service referrals (Carruth, 1973; Hubbard, Santos, & Santos, 1979; Rosin & Glatt, 1971). In addition, some recent data have been collected from research on programs specifically targeting and actively seeking older persons who have alcohol problems (Dupree, Broskowski, & Schonfeld, 1984). A problem with most of these studies, however, is that traditional addictions treatment approaches (where the older person is required to acknowledge a drinking problem and leave the house to attend addictions treatment) seem to attract a very small proportion of older people, and therefore, treatment samples are not likely to be reflective of substance abusers among older persons in general. Only one report of limited circulation (Vermette & Létourneau, 1990) was found concerning an outreach treatment program for older persons. Finally, several studies have examined the factors associated with alcohol problems among older people by surveying caregivers (Hinrichsen, 1984; Israelstam, 1988). Although some of these studies have provided some rich information about alcohol problems among older people, weaknesses have included small sample sizes, lack of systematic data collection, no comparison data (on older people who do not have alcohol problems), and probable sampling bias.

Table 2 summarizes what has been found in previous research concerning the factors associated with alcohol problems among older people. As is evident from Table 2, a number of different methodologies have been employed and a wide variety of factors have been identified. In some studies (Adlaf, Smart, & Jansen, 1989; Barnes, 1982; Brown & Chiang, 1983-84; Carruth, 1973; Meyers et al., 1982; Nakamura et al., 1990; Rathbone-McCuan et al., 1976), comparisons were made between older heavy or problem drinkers and older persons who were not problem drinkers (light or moderate drinkers, abstainers). In others, older-adult heavy or problem drinkers were compared to younger-adult heavy or problem

TABLE 2. Factors Identified in the Literature as Associated with Alcohol Problems Among the Elderly

Factors associated with alcohol problems	Source	Characteristics of study
A. Studies comparing elderly who have alcohol problems to elderly who do not have alcohol problems		
Greater "alienation" (combined score on powerlessness, normlessness, and social isolation).	Rathbone-McCuan, Lohn, Levenson & Hsu (1976)	Interviews with 595 elderly in Baltimore area (220 in community homes, and 38 in high-rise buildings, 232 in nursing homes, and 38 in domiciliary (shelter) residences).
Poorer health among non-drinkers and alcoholics than among normal drinkers and problem drinkers.		
More social support for drinking (i.e., more family and friends who have drinking problems, alcohol served more frequently at social functions).		The brief MAST was used to identify 30 alcoholics. An additional 53 "clinically suspicious" problem drinkers were identified on the basis of responses to the MAST as well as other responses to interview questions.
More likely to report never visiting or being visited by "significant others" (relatives, friends, neighbors).		
More likely to be unable to share important or intimate details of their lives with friends or relatives.		Some additional analyses done using interviews from an additional 53 alcoholics in treatment.
Less satisfaction with social participation.		
No differences between heavy drinking elderly and those who were not heavy drinkers on measures of: life satisfaction, social activities, or health status.	Barnes (1982)	General population survey of 1041 persons in upper New York state. Thirty-one people aged 60 or older were identified as heavy drinkers (consumed 1 or more oz. of absolute alcohol per day). Compared heavy drinkers to others in same age group.
Those with alcohol-related problems reported being less satisfied with their lives. All problem drinkers identified had long-term drinking problems.	Meyers, Hingson, Mucatel, & Goldman (1982)	The data were collected as part of a longitudinal study of adults aged 18 or over in the Boston area. Information was collected relating to

There was no evidence of late onset alcoholism or alcohol abuse caused by stresses of aging.

drinking practices, life problems and life satisfaction. The sample included in the present report consisted of the 928 respondents who were aged 60 or older. Of these, 53% reported that they were abstainers, 26% had less than one drink daily. 22% had one drink or more daily, and 6% had two or more drinks daily. Forty older respondents (4% of the sample) reported having some kind of drinking problem.

Substance abusers were more likely to be currently separated or divorced and to have moved during the prior two years; and less likely to have a relative or good friend living nearby. However, when age and gender were controlled in the analyses, differences in recent moves and availability of friends were no longer significant. Analysis controlling for age and sex found that nonabusers were more likely to be married or widowed and abusers were more likely to be living alone.

Brown & Chiang (1983-84)

The sample was drawn from three sources in the Madison Wisconsin area: a one month survey of all new clients aged 55 or older in three drug abuse agencies (n=21), a one month survey of new admissions age 55 or older to 4 community agencies (n=153), and a random sample of 65 elderly public housing residents. Of the sample from community agencies and elderly housing, 30 (14%) were identified as alcohol and/or drug abusers and 155 were classified as non-abusers (the rest were excluded as uncertain whether they were abusing substances).

Greater alcohol intake and problems associated with lower social fulfillment, greater mastery, greater negative life-events. Also greater alcohol intake was associated with greater negative feelings and greater alcohol problems were associated with lower social support; frequency of alcohol use was associated with better health and more frequent social activity.

Adlaf, Smart, & Jansen (1989)

A sample of 349 individuals from senior citizens apartments. About 5% consumed about 3 drinks daily and about 8% responded positively to at least 2 problem drinking indicators.

TABLE 2 (continued)

Multivariate stepwise discriminant analysis indicated the following variables as significantly identifying severe problem drinkers: unimpaired on activities of daily living; not on digitalis, diuretic, diabetes, or arthritis medications; high school education or less; cohabiting; smoked after age 40; and heavy alcohol intake before age 40.	Nakamura et al. (1990)	The sample was based on a general population interview study conducted in the San Diego area. The sample consisted of 405 people aged 65 or over who had consumed alcohol since age 40.

B. High risk drinkers compared to low risk drinkers across age categories

Higher depression (all age groups)	Warheit & Auth (1984)	General survey of over 4,000 persons on mental health issues. Of the 1,820 in the age group over 50, 42 were designated high risk users (based on reported frequency of intoxication, problems related to drinking, and other variables related to drinking).
Higher anxiety (all age groups except age 18-22).		
Higher psychosocial dysfunction (all age groups except age 18-22).		
More moves (age 18-29, 50+).		
Married, and more likely to feel helpless to deal with family problems (age 18-29, 50+).		
Unmarried, and more likely to indicate lower life satisfaction (age 30-49, 50+).		
More often in hospital (age 30-49, 50+).		
Poorer mental health (age 30-49, 50+).		
More suicide attempts (all age groups).		

C. Elderly alcoholics compared to non-elderly alcoholics

Higher rate of cognitive deficits than younger group.	Blazer, George, Woodbury, Manton, & Jordan (1984)	General survey of 3,796 persons in North Carolina (part of Epidemiologic Catchment Area Project). Of people aged 60 or over, 21 given a current diagnosis of alcohol abuse or dependence, (DIS/DSM III), 117
No significant differences for major depressive disorder, antisocial personality, or sexual difficulties.		

Lower maximum alcohol consumption.

Greater need to drink before breakfast.

Higher proportion wanted to stop drinking but could not.

given a lifetime diagnosis of alcohol abuse or dependence, and 49 reported at least one symptom of alcohol abuse or dependence in prior year- 21 given current diagnosis of alcohol abuse or dependence compared to 85 persons aged 18-59 also given diagnosis of alcohol abuse or dependence.

D. Elderly seen in a special program for late-onset problem drinkers

Characteristics of 48 late-onset elderly problem drinkers:
–few medical problems
–20.8% had been arrested for Driving While Impaired
–poor social networks (less than 1 contact daily with friends or acquaintances)
–mild to moderate anxiety
–mild to moderate guilt
–mild to moderate depression (none to mild using Beck Inventory)
–capable of independent living
–high social competence
–high social interest
–high neatness
–absence of pathology (psychosis, irritability, retardation)
–adequate self-esteem
–generally "internal" on locus of control
–more likely to be steady than binge drinkers
–average consumption on drinking days: 10 drinks
–negative mood state preceded first drink of the day
–most drank at home and alone
–over half had prior treatment

Dupree, Broskowski, & Schonfeld (1984)

48 persons aged 55 or over who were identified as late-onset problem drinkers (onset at age 50 or later) by community agencies and referred to special program for the elderly in Florida community.

TABLE 2. (continued)

E. Elderly males defined by social service agencies as having alcohol problems

Higher ratings than normals on every symptom of distress on a Symptoms of Psychological Distress Checklist.	Carruth (1973)	Interviews with a sample of 63 men aged 49-73 who were defined by a social service or health agency as having a problem related to drinking (63% of the people interviewed had either quit drinking or had been light social drinkers during the months preceding the interview). Ratings on symptoms of Psychological Distress Checklist compared to population norms for normals age 45-74.

F. Elderly identified in clinical practice as having alcohol problems

Characteristics of elderly chronic alcoholics: –usually isolated and alienated from spouse and family –typically suffered from malnutrition and renal and liver disease –all living alone –had used and alienated a lot of agencies –vulnerable to crimes and abuse –widows had actually been "team" alcoholics with alcoholic husbands –three styles of adaptation: withdrawn-depressive, hostile-paranoia, manipulative-deceptive Characteristics of late onset alcohol-related problems: –history of social drinking (or sporadic heavy drinking) –heavy drinking periods often traced to traumatic events (e.g., job loss, widowhood) –guilt –usually drank at home and alone –moderate family contacts –lots of justification for drinking (by both client and family)	Hubbard, Santos, & Santos (1979)	From 250 referrals to a Mental Health Outreach Program for the Elderly, 50 were identified (using case reports) as having alcohol-related problems. Four types of alcohol-related problems were identified: chronic long-term alcoholism (20 cases), onset of alcoholism in later years (12 cases), debilitating interactive effects of alcohol use in old age (11 cases), and victimization of older adults by alcoholics (7 cases).

–a lack of meaningful role involvement and lack of positive self-
concept.

Characteristics of cases who showed
debilitating effects of alcohol:
–used alcohol infrequently or in
small quantities but in dangerous
ways (e.g., while taking
medications)
–frequently appeared to be
functionally senile (from alcohol-
drug interactions) and improved
when abstinent

Precipitating causes (in order of most frequent to least frequent): inveterate drinking, personality factors, bereavement, retirement, loneliness, dementia, infirmity, marital stress	Rosin & Glatt (1971)	Case notes from 103 persons aged 65-92 who were seen at a psychiatric consultation (67) or were referred to a geriatric unit (36) and were assessed as having alcohol-related problems.

Consequences:
–deterioration in physical, mental
or social conditions
–self-neglect
–falls
–excessive incontinence
–confusion aggravated
–paranoid or more aggressive after
drinking
–drinking precipitated family
quarrels or estrangement
–drinking precipitated marriage
break-up

G. Older Persons Seen in Elder-Specific Addictions Treatment program

Characteristics of 48 clients: –79% of women and 58% of men were taking prescribed drugs with a mean use of 3.7 drugs per person –the most commonly used drugs were heart and blood pressure medications and minor tranquilizers. –27% of sample were using minor tranquilizers –60% were current smokers and 21% past smokers	Vermette & Létourneau (1990)	23 females and 25 males aged 60 and over receiving treatment from an outreach program for older adult substance abusers.

TABLE 2. (continued)

−82% of clients reported at least
one problem in cognitive functioning
−55% of clients reported at least one
problem in activities of daily living

H. Data from addictions workers who treat elderly persons who have alcohol problems

Less likely to have job problems, problems with friends and neighbors, or problems with police (compared to younger clients). Often exhibited acute or long-term medical problems.	Hinrichsen (1984)	Site visits to 40 alcoholism treatment programs plus 5 special programs for the elderly. Interviewed staff about characteristics of people aged 60 and over in the program.
Factors believed to be related to excessive drinking among seniors (rated significantly more likely than for the general population): −feel lonely −feel loss of loved ones −no role in society −bored −rejection by families −loss of physical well-being −not prepared for life −aging changes −no social status −fear of death −feel society is hostile −society is hostile	Israelstam (1988)	A survey of alcohol intervention workers concerning the factors that they perceived to be associated with alcohol abuse among retired seniors (aged 65+) compared to the general population.

drinkers (Blazer et al., 1984; Hinrichsen, 1984). Warheit and Auth (1984) compared high-risk drinkers to low-risk drinkers across different age groups, and Israelstam (1988) compared older people to the general population. Studies comparing older alcohol abusers to abusers in other age groups can provide useful information for differentiating factors that may be particularly associated with alcohol problems among older people (as compared with factors associated with alcohol problems for all age groups); on the other hand, comparisons of alcohol abusers to nonabusers among older persons can help to differentiate factors that are associated with alcohol problems as opposed to factors that are generally related to aging.

Finally, a group of studies (Dupree, Broskowski, & Schonfeld, 1984; Hubbard, Santos, & Santos, 1979; Rosin & Glatt, 1971; Vermette & Létourneau, 1990) examine alcohol problems among older persons without using a comparison group. While this approach does not address how older problem drinkers might be different from other problem drinkers or from older people who do not have substance problems, this exploratory descriptive approach has some advantages. On a practical level, an understanding of the problem area is probably necessary for effective treatment, but knowledge of the extent to which these problems are unique to this population is probably not required. Perhaps the major advantage of this approach is that it allows the greatest latitude in choosing variables that are relevant to the target population and is, therefore, most likely to identify the critical variables or dimensions relevant to substance abuse among this population. Some of the studies that have compared older to younger problem drinkers have been of limited usefulness, because the variables chosen tended to be more relevant to younger drinkers than to older drinkers (because the role of alcohol in the life of the retired older person living alone may be quite different from the role of alcohol for a married, employed, younger person). The importance of data from uncontrolled clinical studies cannot be overlooked, since much of the current capability to conduct controlled research on alcoholics generally was based on the descriptive data collected in early clinical studies. The gathering of clinical observations and descriptive data on older substance abusers is a necessary step in understanding this particular population.

OLDER PROBLEM DRINKERS COMPARED TO OLDER PEOPLE WHO DO NOT HAVE ALCOHOL PROBLEMS

Based on the literature described in Table 2, the following factors were found to be associated with problem drinking among older people, compared to older persons who do not have alcohol problems: greater alienation; higher depression; higher anxiety; greater psychosocial dysfunction; poorer mental health; greater levels of symptoms of psychological distress; more transience; on fewer medications for heart, blood pressure, diabetes, or arthritis; more likely to have smoked after age 40; more likely to have heavy intake of alcohol before age 40; more likely to be unimpaired on activities of daily living; more social support for drinking; fewer significant social contacts; fewer intimate relationships; less social fulfillment and social support; more helpless in family relationships; more suicide attempts; less satisfaction with social participation; lower life satisfaction (found by Meyers et al., 1992, and by Warheit & Auth, 1984, but no difference in life satisfaction or social activities found by Barnes, 1982); and poorer health and more often in the hospital (found by Meyers et al., and by Warheit & Auth, but no difference in health status found by Barnes or by Adlaf, Smart, & Jansen, 1989).

OLDER PROBLEM DRINKERS COMPARED TO YOUNGER PROBLEM DRINKERS

Compared to problem drinkers in other age groups, the following factors were identified with problem drinking among older persons: higher rate of cognitive deficits, lower maximum alcohol consumption, greater need to drink before breakfast, higher proportion who wanted to stop drinking but could not, less likely to have job problems, less likely to have problems with friends and neighbors, less likely to have problems with police, and more likely to have acute or long-term medical problems. However, older problem drinkers were not found to be significantly different from other adult problem drinkers in terms of frequency of major depressive disorders, antisocial personality, or sexual difficulties. Finally, alcohol treatment workers indicated that older people were more likely than the general population to drink excessively in response to loneliness, bereavement, boredom, deterioration of physical health, rejection by families and society, changes with aging, and a lack of role or status in society.

DESCRIPTIONS OF OLDER PROBLEM DRINKERS IN NONCOMPARATIVE STUDIES

The following characteristics of elderly persons who have alcohol problems were identified in the noncomparative studies:

1. Factors that applied *generally to alcohol problems* in this age group included those described as *precipitating* factors–inveterate drinking, personality factors, bereavement, retirement, loneliness, dementia, infirmity, and marital stress; and those described as *consequences of heavy drinking*–deterioration in physical, mental, or social conditions; self-neglect; falls; excessive incontinence; and confusion.

2. Characteristics of *late-onset older problem drinkers*–generally well-functioning with few major psychosocial problems, poor social networks, more likely to be steady drinkers than binge drinkers, average consumption on typical drinking day of ten drinks, negative mood state preceded first drink of day, most drank at home and alone, over half had had prior treatment, usually had a history of social drinking (or sporadic heavier drinking), heavy drinking periods often traced to traumatic events (e.g., job loss, widowhood), expressed guilt, moderate level of family contacts, a lack of meaningful role involvement, and lack of positive self-concept (identified by Hubbard, Santos, & Santos, 1979; but self-esteem judged adequate by Dupree, Broskowski, & Schonfeld, 1984).

3. Characteristics of *older chronic alcoholics*–usually socially isolated, alienated from family, physical health problems, living alone, had used and alienated a lot of agencies, vulnerable to crimes and abuse, and widows had developed excessive drinking with alcoholic husbands.

DISCUSSION

There are a few themes or issues that seem to emerge from this diffuse list of factors. One issue is that different factors may be associated with older problem drinkers depending on whether they are chronic lifetime alcohol abusers or late-onset heavy drinkers. Chronic alcoholics appeared to be more deteriorated in physical health, more isolated, and possibly exhibiting more mental health problems. Late-onset drinkers, on the other hand, seemed to be less deteriorated (physically and mentally) than the chronic drinkers, but shared some of the social isolation of long-time alcohol abusers. The late-onset problem drinkers also seemed to demonstrate a more reactive drinking pattern (possibly one established earlier in life during periods of high stress). These differences between early- and late-onset older drinkers were confirmed by Atkinson et al. (1985), who compared 14 early-onset cases to 22 late-onset cases on a number of variables measured retrospectively using a sample from a Veterans Administration alcohol treatment clinic. They found that early-onset clients were more likely to report family alcoholism, more likely to have been charged with alcohol-related offenses, and more likely to have been jailed for alcohol use. However, Atkinson et al. defined late onset as after age 40, which is much younger than late onset is typically defined in most other studies (especially when the late-onset drinking is seen to be related to bereavement, retirement, and other variables related to being "elderly"). Finally, Hubbard, Santos, and Santos (1979) identified a third type of older problem drinker (dangerous alcohol use because of drug interactions) who tended to have little in common with chronic or late-onset problem drinkers.

The existence of groups of older alcoholics who are quite different from one another has some implications for interpreting research on alcohol and older people. Factors identified in any single study may well depend on the weighting of different types of drinkers within the sample of older problem drinkers. This may be especially relevant for comparative studies where elderly problem drinkers are treated as a homogeneous (or at least meaningful) group compared to other arbitrarily defined groups. For example, the chronic alcoholic who is 70 may have more in common with the chronic alcoholic who is 45 than with the late-onset problem drinker who is 70.

Another problem for studies of alcohol abusers is how to categorize those who have had alcohol problems at one time but no longer have problems (logically, this would be more problematic for older samples who have a longer personal history during which alcohol problems may have developed and been resolved). Blazer et al. (1984) found 21 people over age 60 who were diagnosed as currently abusing alcohol, but 117 who were diagnosed as demonstrating alcohol abuse or dependence at some time during their lives. In comparing older problem drinkers to elderly persons who do not have alcohol problems, the group who previously had problems would need to be identified and analyzed separately.

Table 3 summarizes findings from the previous literature organized by general life areas. In terms of *alcohol use and problems*, older alcohol abusers are more likely than nonabusers to have a history of heavier drinking and to have a social context supportive of drinking. Older alcohol abusers drink less on a single occasion than younger abusers, but are more likely to drink in the morning. Loss of relationships due to drinking and inappropriate behavior while drinking have been observed among older alcohol abusers. Regarding *use of other drugs*, older alcohol abusers are more likely than nonabusers to smoke, and are likely to show a high rate of use of minor tranquilizers.

Physical health is likely to be poor among older alcohol abusers, although not all studies have found higher rates of physical health problems among older alcohol abusers compared to nonabusers. The findings are more consistent that older alcohol abusers have poorer mental/emotional health than older people who do not abuse alcohol. However, older alcohol abusers have not been found to have higher rates of psychiatric diagnoses than younger abusers. Although self-neglect has been observed among older alcohol abusers, one study of older problem drinkers found that problem drinkers were less likely to be impaired on activities of daily living.

A number of studies have found that older alcohol abusers experience greater *social* isolation, fewer significant or intimate relationships, and lower life satisfaction than nonabusing elderly. Compared to younger alcohol abusers, older abusers seem to have less problems with friends and neighbors, which supports the interpretation that problems with social isolation occur more frequently than problems involving altercations with others.

Finally, older alcohol abusers are less likely than their younger counterparts to have *economic/employment* problems or *legal* problems; however, they are more likely than older nonabusers to move frequently, and to feel helpless in family relationships.

TABLE 3. Summary of the Literature on Factors Associated with Alcohol Problems Among the Elderly[a] by Life Area

Life Areas	Factors associated with alcohol problems among the elderly
Alcohol use/problems	–more likely to have been a heavy drinker before age 40(E) –more social support for drinking (E) –lower maximum alcohol consumption (A) –greater need to drink before breakfast (A) –higher proportion who wanted to stop drinking but could not (A) –paranoid or more aggressive after drinking –drinking precipitated family quarrels or estrangement –drinking precipitated marriage break-up
Drug use	–more likely to have smoked since age 40 (E) –high rate of use of minor tranquilizers
Physical health	–poorer health (E) –no difference on health status (E) –more often in hospital[b] (E) –more likely to have acute or long-term medical problems (A) –falls –infirmity –loss of physical well-being –less likely to be on medications for heart, blood pressure, diabetes, or arthritis (E)
Mental/emotional health	–higher depression[b] (E) –higher anxiety[b] (E) –greater psychosocial dysfunction[b] (E) –greater levels of symptoms of psychological distress (E) –more suicide attempts[b] (E) –poorer mental health[b] (E) –more cognitive deficits (E) –not different on diagnosis of major depressive disorder (A) –not different on diagnosis of antisocial personality (A) –not different on diagnosis of sexual difficulties (A) –bereavement –dementia –confusion –fears of death
Activities of daily living/nutrition	–self-neglect –more likely to be unimpaired on activities of daily living (E)

Social/leisure/family	–greater alienation (E)
	–fewer significant social contacts (E)
	–fewer intimate relationships (E)
	–lower satisfaction with social participation (E)
	–lower life satisfaction[b] (E)
	–no different on life satisfaction (E)
	–no difference on social activities (E)
	–less likely to have problems with friends and neighbors (A)
	–loneliness
	–no role in society
	–bored
	–no social status
	–feel society is hostile/society *is* hostile
Economic/employment	–less likely to have job problems (A)
Accommodation	–more moves[b] (E)
Relationship with spouse	–more likely to feel helpless to deal with family problems[b] (E)
Legal	–less likely to have problem with police (A)

Note: E - indicates comparisons of elderly alcohol abusers to elderly who do not have alcohol problems; A - indicates comparisons to non-elderly who have alcohol problems; where there is no letter following the factor, the factor describes elderly substance abusers without reference to a comparison group.

[a] Factors differentiating late-onset versus early-onset alcohol abusers are not included in this table.

[b] These factors were found associated with alcohol abuse regardless of age (i.e., differentiated alcohol abusers from nonabusers among elderly but also among some other age groups).

Chapter 6

Problem Areas Identified Among COPA Clients

The present research adopted an exploratory approach to investigating the factors associated with substance abuse in a clinical sample of older substance abusers (without comparison to other populations). As described previously, the noncomparative approach has a number of advantages–principal among them is that the approach is more likely to identify critical dimensions as well as various subtypes of the target population. Previous research has only begun the process of describing alcohol problems among older people. It is apparent that increasingly focused descriptive research is required in order to mount meaningful large scale comparative studies. The COPA evaluation offers some unique advantages in this endeavor. First, many of the previous noncomparative studies did not collect data systematically, and the findings were more reflective of clinical insight than of objective data analyses. The COPA evaluation included systematic objective data collection, in addition to a less objective approach using a case study method. Second, samples in previous studies, using treatment populations from traditional addictions treatment programs or from mental health or psychiatric populations, were likely to be biased since older people rarely attend traditional addictions treatment. Therefore, those who do attend traditional addictions treatment programs are likely not representative of the population of older people who have alcohol problems. The COPA Project is different from traditional addictions treatment programs in two important ways: (1) it uses outreach methods, and (2) it does not require that the person being helped acknowledge that he or she has an alcohol problem. Many of the people treated by the program would not have attended traditional programs;[1] therefore, the elderly seen by COPA are probably more representative of the population who have alcohol problems than are clients in traditional addictions treatment programs.

The data recording process for the COPA evaluation was organized by the following life areas: alcohol use/problems, drug use (primarily prescription drug use), physical health, emotional health, cognitive/mental health, activities of daily living, social contacts (including family), leisure activities, nutrition, economic well-being, accommodation, relationship with spouse, and legal status. In order to facilitate comparison of COPA data with findings from the literature, the same life areas were used to summarize the factors that were identified in the literature as being associated with alcohol problems among the elderly (previously shown in Table 3).

As described in Chapter 4, there were several program factors that affected the data collection. First, the primary mandate of the program was treatment, not research. While research was perceived to be an important aspect of the program, care was taken that the data collection did not intrude on clients or hamper the treatment process. The lower priority of the research resulted in a high rate of missing data at assessment. Second, the approach of the program was nonconfrontational. This meant that help was provided to clients in the areas which they defined as problematic, and substance problems were addressed directly only when and if the client chose. Thus, during initial contacts, clients could be quite evasive about substance use and related problems. From a clinical perspective, this was not perceived to be a problem. However, from a research perspective, it was important to try to make a valid assessment of

---

1. Repeated surveys of Ontario addictions programs, one in 1983 (Rush & Timney, 1983) the second in 1986 (Rush & Ekdahl, 1987), demonstrated the increased penetration accomplished by the COPA approach. Between the survey of 1983 and that of 1986, COPA was established, as was another similar program in a different city. These two programs appeared to cause a dramatic rise in the proportion of older people seen in community-based, nonresidential addictions programs. While proportions in other types of programs (e.g., hospital-based residential, community-based residential, etc.) remained about the same (with slight increases in the over-65 age group), the number of people over age 65 seen by community-based, nonresidential programs rose from 67 (1.0 percent of cases in that type of program) in 1983, to 247 (7.7 percent of cases) in 1986.

the client's status at entry into the program in order to be able to assess the impact of the program on the client. Therefore, in addition to self-report from the client, two other procedures were included in the data collection in order to estimate the client's status in various life areas: (1) recording of data from other sources (e.g., the referring agency, family members), and (2) recording the perceptions of the COPA worker (at assessment and during the treatment process). In this way, several types of information were available to describe the nature of problems among elderly persons treated at COPA. In addition, the study included several levels of data collection and analyses: initial assessment of clients at entry into the program, monitoring of clients' progress during treatment, and selected cases studies.

In this section, results will be presented using variables from the various data collection strategies. Descriptions of the extent of problems in each life area will be presented according to (1) data collected at assessment (n = 91) and (2) data collected during the treatment process (n = 56), and (3) findings from the case studies, which are referred to in the discussion of the findings throughout this chapter. Since somewhat different aspects of each life area were examined by the different data collection procedures, these three sources of information present slightly different (but generally converging) perspectives of the factors associated with substance problems among older persons who were seen at the COPA program. The assessment and treatment samples were very similar; however, the case study sample included only those who had clear alcohol problems, and tended to contain a larger proportion of heavier drinkers than the other two samples.

Clients could be admitted to COPA with alcohol problems, drug problems, or both alcohol and drug problems. Of the 56 clients included in the treatment sample, 21 (38 percent) were rated as having moderate to extreme alcohol problems and no drug problems at assessment, 21 (38 percent) were rated as having both alcohol and drug problems, and 6 (11 percent) were rated as having drug problems only. For the remaining 8 cases (14 percent), no ratings on these life areas were made at assessment.

OVERALL RATINGS OF PROBLEMS
IN EACH LIFE AREA

Table 4 shows the problem areas identified at assessment for all clients assessed, and for the treatment subsample. (Table 5, presented later, will show the extent to which specific life areas were problematic during the treatment process as reflected by information from client monitoring.) As shown in Table 4, there were few significant differences in the overall ratings between the total sample assessed and the treatment subsample. The major difference between the subsample and the total sample was that the treatment subsample tended to have slightly higher ratings of alcohol and drug problems.

Regardless of sample, however, there were large discrepancies between ratings by the clients themselves about how much they were worried about particular life areas, compared to the counselor's rating of problem severity for the life areas (see Table 4). Overall, using the client's worry about an area as a measure of extent of problems gives a much lower problem rate for most life areas, compared to problem rates based on the counselor's rating of problem severity. The greatest discrepancies were identified for the following: alcohol use, drug use, emotional/mental health, social relationships, and leisure activities. It is likely that some of the discrepancies in the present research were due to the outreach nature of the program–that is, few clients were actually seeking addictions treatment, and although some wanted help with specific problems (e.g., housing), many were not interested in receiving general counseling, particularly regarding their alcohol consumption. In addition, a client's lack of concern regarding some life areas (particularly alcohol use) might be attributable to denial. It is also likely that most clients were referred to COPA at a crisis point in their lives, and the difference between the counselor's rating and the client's rating might reflect different perspectives: namely, the counselor rated the clients on their status at the time they were referred. If a crisis had precipitated the referral, the client's problems might have been at an unusually severe level. On the other hand, the client may have taken a longer perspective and rated problems in a particular life area according to a usual level of

TABLE 4. Summary Ratings for Each Life Area (Assessment)

Life area	Proportion of clients who rated this life area a moderate to extreme worry[a]		Proportion of clients for whom the COPA counselor rated the client's need for assistance in this area as moderate to extreme[b]	
	All assessed cases (n=91)	Treated cases analyzed (n=56)	All assessed cases (n=91)	Treated cases analyzed (n=56)
Alcohol use	40.8 (n=71)	51.2 (n=41)	86.4 (n=81)	91.3 (n=46)*
Drug use	15.1 (n=53)	21.1 (n=38)*	45.2 (n=73)	55.1 (n=49)*
Physical health	54.0 (n=87)	44.9 (n=49)	60.5 (n=76)	62.0 (n=50)
Emotional/mental health	37.8 (n=82)	37.0 (n=46)	86.4 (n=88)	88.0 (n=50)
Activities of daily living	44.4 (n=72)	46.9 (n=49)	63.2 (n=76)	68.0 (n=50)
Social relationships	21.1 (n=76)	17.8 (n=45)	69.7 (n=89)	64.0 (n=50)
Leisure activities	28.2 (n=85)	23.9 (n=46)	75.0 (n=88)	75.5 (n=49)
Family relationships	36.8 (n=76)	37.8 (n=45)	51.1 (n=90)	60.0 (n=50)
Nutrition	20.3 (n=69)	24.5 (n=49)	41.3 (n=75)	44.0 (n=50)
Economic status	39.5 (n=81)	36.7 (n=49)	24.4 (n=82)	26.5 (n=49)
Accommodation status	40.2 (n=82)	39.1 (n=46)	53.4 (n=88)	58.0 (n=50)
Employment status	16.4 (n=55)	15.4 (n=39)	24.1 (n=83)	22.4 (n=49)
Relationship with spouse	40.0 (n=65)	37.8 (n=37)	44.6 (n=83)	45.7 (n=46)
Legal status	16.1 (n=56)	11.8 (n=34)	10.2 (n=88)	12.0 (n=50)

[a] Clients who indicated that this life area was a moderate to extreme worry were defined as those whose average score was 2.5 or more for two questions on how worried the client had been about the life area and how important it was to the client to get help for the life area (scale: 1-not at all, 2-slightly, 3-moderately, 4-considerably, 5-extremely).

[b] Scale for rating client's need for assistance consisted of 1-client strength/support system, 2-no real problem, assistance probably not indicated, 3-slight problem, assistance probably not necessary, 4-moderate problem, some assistance indicated, 5-considerable problem, assistance necessary, 6-extreme crisis, immediate assistance essential.

problems, rather than problems at the time of the crisis that precipitated entry to COPA. Another explanation might be that the low concern expressed by clients about specific life areas such as social relationships and leisure activities may reflect a fatalism and hopelessness about aging–that is, a belief by the client that old age is inevitably lonely. Alternatively, alcohol abuse by the clients may have impaired their ability to judge the severity of problems in some life areas. For whatever reasons, the profile of problems associated with substance abuse among the elderly is less severe when rated by the client than when rated by the counselor.

Data on client status during the treatment process (Table 5) provide some basis for interpreting the counselor's rating of the severity of the client's problems. Note that exact comparison with the initial severity rating is not possible on most variables, as slightly different items were used to measure ongoing status than were used on the initial assessment form. This difference in approach was attributable to the different functions of the assessment ratings and the monitoring ratings. Whereas the assessment form documented the client's general status at the time of entry into the program, ratings made during the treatment process were chosen to reflect the variability observed during weekly contacts. For example, as part of monitoring, alcohol use/consumption was measured using two items: recent pattern of consumption (abstinent, light, heavy, or problem), and recent frequency of drinking (none, occasional, frequent, daily). The assessment ratings, on the other hand, were intended to provide a more stable reflection of the client's status at entry into the program. Nevertheless, comparing the extent of problems in each life area as measured by the two methods provides some cross-validation of the two approaches in estimating extent of problems among an elderly sample of substance abusers. In general, for most life areas (with the exception of physical health and social/leisure activities), the proportion of clients whose *most problematic rating* during treatment fell into the problem range corresponded fairly closely with the proportion whose need for assistance was ranked moderate to severe at the time of assessment. *Average ratings* over the treatment process, however, tended to indicate lower proportions of clients with problems than did the assessment ratings. The lower problem rates observed in the average ratings over treatment might reflect the alleviation of a

TABLE 5. Extent of Problems in Each Life Area Identified During the Treatment Process

Life area	Variable	Proportion whose most problematic rating fell into problem range	Proportion whose average rating fell into problem range	Proportion whose least problematic rating fell into problem range
Alcohol use	rating of alcohol consumption since last contact (n=47)	78.7	29.8	14.9
	frequency of drinking according to client (n=53)	81.1	44.3	18.9
Drug use	status of current drug use (n=39)	41.0	7.7	5.1
Physical health	physical health status (n=56)	80.4	55.4	12.5
Emotional health	emotional health status (n=56)	87.5	60.7	7.1
Mental/cognitive	mental/cognitive health status (n=56)	62.5	23.2	3.6
Activities of daily living	personal hygiene (n=56)	53.6	12.5	3.6
	care of clothing (n=56)	50.0	16.1	5.4
	care of living quarters (n=55)	41.8	14.5	5.5

TABLE 5 (continued)

Life area	Variable	Proportion whose most problematic rating fell into problem range	Proportion whose average rating fell into problem range	Proportion whose least problematic fell into problem range
Social/leisure	extent of social contacts (n=41)	82.9	58.5	19.5
	extent of leisure activities (n=41)	87.8	73.2	31.7
Nutrition	adequacy of diet (n=38)	52.6	13.2	5.3
	appetite (n=38)	63.2	15.8	2.6
Economic	economic status (n=44)	43.2	11.4	2.3
Accommodation	accommodation status (n=47)	59.6	34.0	14.9
Spouse	relationship with spouse/ significant other (n=34)	44.1	17.6	5.9
Legal	current legal status (n=41)	26.8	4.9	2.4

Note: Problem range for each variable is defined in Appendix A.

crisis situation at entry to the program, as well as the client's improvement while in the program.

In Table 6, the counselors' ratings were used to rank life areas in terms of prevalence of problems. Using either the counselor's problem rating at assessment or the most problematic rating during treatment to estimate the prevalence of problems in each life area, the life areas with the highest proportion of problems (more than 75 percent of clients) were alcohol use, emotional health, leisure activities, social relationships, and physical health; the life areas showing moderate prevalence (50-75 percent) were activities of daily living, nutrition, cognitive/mental health, family relationships, accommodation, and drug use; and areas with lower prevalence of problems (less than 50 percent of clients) were relationship with spouse, economic status, legal status, and employment status. Table 6 also contains estimates of problem prevalence using two other measures of problems: (1) the counselor's average rating of the client's ongoing status in each life area over the time the client was in treatment, and (2) the client's ratings of concern about the life area at the time of assessment. As might be expected, *average* ratings by the counselors indicated lower prevalence estimates than estimates based on the *most problematic* rating. Nevertheless, the rank ordering of life areas according to prevalence estimates is roughly the same whether the most problematic rating or the average rating was used.

However, prevalence rates based on the *client's concern* about the life area showed a considerably different pattern. Not only were these estimates of problem prevalence much lower than estimates based on ratings made by the counselor (as was apparent in Table 4), but the rank ordering of life areas according to the client's concern was considerably different. Concern by clients was highest for alcohol use, activities of daily living, physical health, accommodation, family and marital relationships, emotional health, and economic status.

Summary

Taking these several sources of information into account, there is consistent evidence that among older people who have substance problems, the life areas (other than alcohol use) most likely to demonstrate high rates of problems are physical health, emotional

TABLE 6. Comparison of Different Methods of Estimating Prevalence of Problems[a] in Each Life Area

	Proportion of clients whose rating at assessment was in the problem range (rank in parentheses)	Proportion of clients whose most problematic rating during treatment was in the problem range (rank in parentheses)	Proportion of clients whose average rating during treatment was in the problem range (rank in parentheses)	Proportion of clients whose rating of concern about that life area at assessment was in the problem range (rank in parentheses)
More than 75% of clients identified as having problems at assessment or during treatment:				
alcohol use	91.3 (1)	78.7/81.1 (4)	29.8/44.3 (5)	51.2 (1)
emotional health	88.0 (2)	87.5 (2)	60.7 (2)	37.0 (6)
leisure activities	75.5 (3)	87.8 (1)	73.2 (1)	23.9 (9)
social relationships	64.0 (5)	82.9 (3)	58.5 (3)	17.8 (11)
physical health	62.0 (6)	80.4 (5)	55.4 (4)	44.9 (3)
50% to 75% of clients identified as having problems at assessment or during treatment:				
activities of daily living	68.4 (4)	41.8/53.6[b] (9)	12.5/16.1[b] (9)	46.9 (2)
nutrition	44.0 (11)	52.6/63.2[b] (6)	13.2/15.8[b] (10)	24.5 (8)
cognitive/mental health	-- --	62.5 (7)	23.2 (7)	-- --
family relationships	60.0 (7)	-- --	-- --	37.8 (5)
accommodation	58.0 (8)	59.6 (8)	34.0 (6)	39.1 (4)
drug use	55.1 (9)	41.0 (12)	7.7 (12)	21.1 (10)
Less than 50% of clients identified as having problems at assessment or during treatment:				
relationship with spouse	45.7 (10)	44.1 (10)	17.6 (8)	37.8 (5)
economic status	26.5 (12)	43.2 (11)	11.4 (13)	36.7 (7)
legal status	12.0 (14)	26.8 (13)	4.9 (13)	11.8 (13)
employment status	22.4 (13)	-- --	-- --	15.4 (12)

[a]Ratings are for cases in the treatment sample (n=56)
[b]Ratings on several aspects of daily living and nutrition rather than global ratings

health, activities of daily living, accommodation, and family relationships. Problems in leisure activities and social relationships showed high prevalence according to ratings made by the counselors, but low prevalence when based on concern expressed by the clients. On the other hand, relationship with spouse and economic status showed fairly high ranking based on concern by clients, but lower ranking based on counselors' ratings. Problems regarding legal status and employment were of low prevalence among this group of older substance abusers, regardless of the measure used to estimate prevalence.

The following sections provide more detailed descriptions of the nature of client problems in each life area using variables from the initial assessment, the treatment process, and subjective judgments made on the basis of the case studies.

ALCOHOL CONSUMPTION AND PROBLEMS

The assessment instrument included a large number of items on alcohol consumption and problems, but given the nature of the program (outreach, nonconfrontational), complete information was not available for most clients. Information was collected from the client and, where possible, from another source familiar with the client's drinking. Items that seemed to have the best response rate and greatest interpretability are presented in Table 7. As is evident from this table, the extent of alcohol problems appeared to be much lower when based on self-report by clients than when information from other sources was used. To some degree, the lower rates using only self-report data reflect missing data (i.e., the client was generally unwilling or unable to discuss alcohol use) as much as outright denial of particular use patterns or problems. In addition, the higher rates of alcohol problems observed when information from other sources was used may be somewhat inflated by the method for calculating these ratings. For example, if a client reported that drinking had not been affecting his moods but his wife said that it had, in the present analyses, this variable was rated as a problem for that person based on the other source (even though it was in contradiction to the client's self-report).

TABLE 7. Alcohol Use - Data Recorded at Assessment

Variable	Based on self-report	Based on self-report plus additional information from others[a]	
Proportion of clients who drank daily or nearly every day	50.8	74.6	(n=59)
Proportion who reported usually drinking 5 or more drinks on one occasion	17.8 (n=45)		
Proportion who reported ever drinking 5 or more drinks on one occasion	34.9 (n=44)		
Proportion for whom drinking seemed to be affecting health	40.1	82.8	(n=64)
Proportion for whom drinking seemed to be affecting walking	23.4	56.3	(n=64)
Proportion for whom drinking seemed to be affecting the client's moods	20.3	62.5	(n=64)
Proportion for whom drinking seemed to be affecting memory/ability to think	21.9	53.1	(n=64)
Proportion for whom drinking seemed to be affecting getting along with people	10.9	46.9	(n=64)
Proportion for whom it was believed that cutting down on drinking would improve health, mood, etc.	35.9	62.5	(n=64)
Proportion who recently experienced dependence symptoms from drinking	18.3	56.7	(n=60)
Proportion who had major chronic health problems related to alcohol consumption	15.0	60.0	(n=60)
Proportion who had major problems in their pattern of drinking	21.7	68.3	(n=60)
Proportion who had major behavioral problems from alcohol	20.0	70.0	(n=60)
Proportion who had major problems with side effects from alcohol use	25.0	70.0	(n=60)

Variable	Based on self-report	Based on self-report plus additional information from others[a]
Proportion who reported prior admissions to detox		
–for alcohol use	13.3 (n=75)	
–for drug use	2.7 (n=75)	
–for alcohol and drug use	0.0 (n=75)	
Proportion who reported previous addictions treatment (other than detox)		
–for alcohol use	38.7 (n=75)	
–for drug use	6.7 (n=75)	
–for alcohol and drug use	1.3 (n=75)	
Proportion who reported that they would not be wiling to reduce their alcohol consumption	23.1 (n=52)	
Proportion who denied excessive consumption of alcohol	78.8 (n=66)	
Proportion who denied negative consequences of alcohol consumption	84.8 (n=66)	
Proportion who reported that alcohol use had made their lives somewhat or much worse	49.3 (n=69)	

[a] Where possible, information from sources other than the client was included in the assessment data. Frequently, information from other sources indicated heavier drinking and more drinking problems than were reported by the client. For example, where frequency of drinking was reported both by the client and by another source, in 22 cases the other source reported more frequent drinking by the client than the client had reported, in 9 cases the report was the same for the client and the other source, and in 1 case the other source reported less frequent drinking by the client than the client had reported. For variables where information from other sources was recorded, the number of cases on which proportions were based consisted of all cases where there was information from either the client, another source, or both. If either the client or the other source indicated a problem, this was recorded as a problem even if this contradicted one of the informants.

It is also apparent from Table 7, that in many cases, detailed information about the alcohol use and problems of clients was not available at assessment. For some clients, an accurate picture of alcohol problems did not emerge until well into the treatment process, and for other clients, it was never determined exactly how much they drank. Based on the available data from all sources of information, several aspects of alcohol consumption and problems will be discussed in the following sections. These include: extent of denial, stage of life when problem drinking began, consumption patterns, and types of problems.

Extent of Denial

The assessment data indicated a clear pattern of clients seeing themselves as drinking less and experiencing less problems from alcohol than was perceived by others (including the counselor). Data on extent of denial were also collected as part of monitoring during treatment. At some point in the treatment process, 54 percent of those who exhibited alcohol problems were rated as completely denying or avoiding the topic of their own alcohol consumption, and 64 percent were rated as completely denying or avoiding the topic of their own alcohol problems.

The monitoring forms also permitted the counselor to record any signs of alcohol consumption exhibited by the client during contacts with the counselor. These results are presented in Table 8. At least once during the treatment process, over 60 percent of clients exhibited at least one sign of having recently consumed alcohol. The most common signs were that the client's mood suggested prior drinking, alcohol was detected on the client's breath, and the client's appearance suggested prior drinking. These figures indicate a fairly large role of alcohol in the lives of many clients, since clients usually knew in advance when they would be seeing the counselor and most attempted to restrict their alcohol consumption on these occasions.

Finally, from information available in the 36 case studies, it was judged that 49 percent of clients (of the 35 clients for whom judgments were made) were generally open about their alcohol consumption, 20 percent were open but probably underreporting, and 31 percent were evasive or denied consumption (although their behavior or information from other sources indicated heavy or problem drinking).

Stage of Life When Problem Drinking Began

Identifying when problem drinking began was more problematic than might have been expected. No single assessment question seemed to capture this variable accurately. In addition, the case studies suggested that initial information about this was often inaccurate. For example, a client might report at assessment that he began drinking heavily when his wife died. However, it sometimes emerged during the treatment process, that, in fact, this client had a long history of heavy drinking and drinking-related problems. Thus, the

TABLE 8. Signs of Alcohol Consumption Observed During Visit with Client

Sign of alcohol consumption	Number and proportion of clients who exhibited this sign during the treatment process	
Client's mood suggests prior drinking	30	(54%)
Alcohol on client's breath	23	(41%)
Client's appearance suggests prior drinking	20	(36%)
Client's speech indicates probable drinking	17	(30%)
Client exhibiting physical or emotional problems related to recent drinking	17	(30%)
Client's gait or balance indicates problem drinking	16	(29%)
Empties visible in client's living quarters	14	(25%)
Client consuming alcoholic beverage (or probable alcoholic beverage)	12	(21%)
Client's behavior or mental status indicates probable drinking	11	(20%)
Client clearly intoxicated/passed out	11	(20%)
Client has hangover symptoms/tremors	6	(11%)
Other signs	8	(14%)

Note: n = 56

most accurate estimate of time of onset seemed to be available from the case studies (which were able to examine all evidence about the client). Sufficient information to make a judgment as to when problem drinking had begun was available for 29 of the 36 cases analyzed. Of these, 69 percent appeared to have begun heavy or problem drinking in early to middle adulthood, 17 percent seemed to have begun in middle-age, and 14 percent appeared to have begun in later years (i.e., past 65 years of age or post-retirement).

Consumption Patterns

From Table 7, it appeared that at the time of admission, 50 percent (self-report) to 75 percent (including report by others) of the clients were drinking alcohol every day or nearly every day. However, usual and maximum consumption (as reported by clients at assessment) seemed to be quite low, with only 18 percent reporting *usually* drinking five or more drinks on one occasion, and only 35 percent reporting *ever* drinking five or more drinks on one occasion. The monitoring data indicated that these estimates likely reflected underreporting.

The most reliable estimates of consumption from the monitoring data seemed to be the estimates made by the counselor of the client's average daily consumption during the previous week. For the 53 cases (out of 56) on which some data were available concerning average consumption, the *maximum average consumption* reported by the case workers for each client resulted in the following: zero drinks per day–32 percent of clients (including clients who began abstaining at entry into COPA or sometime previous to admission to COPA); 1-4 drinks per day–30 percent of clients; and five or more drinks per day–38 percent of clients. Since some of those who abstained or drank lightly during treatment at COPA were likely to have drunk heavily in the past, these data indicate higher rates of high-volume drinking (five or more drinks) than admitted to at assessment.

Types of Drinking-Related Problems

Based on information recorded at the time of assessment (Table 7), the most frequent drinking-related problem reported by clients as well as others was the effect of drinking on the client's physical health (40 percent, self-report; 83 percent, report by self and other). Other problems from drinking were reported by 11 percent to 70 percent of clients depending on the type of problem and whether the rating was based only on self-report by the client or included information from other sources. In addition, about half of the clients indicated that drinking had made their lives somewhat worse or much worse (the other half reporting that drinking had no effect on their lives, or made their lives better).

Related to this topic, one of the more interesting findings from the case studies was the extent to which major problems in life areas appeared to occur only during periods of binging or heavy drinking. According to case study ratings, major problems that occurred *only* during periods of heavy drinking accounted for over 50 percent of the cases who had major problems in the following life areas: psychiatric problems (6/11, or 55 percent of those who had major problems in this area), cognitive problems (9/11, or 82 percent), physical health problems (15/25, or 60 percent), problems with activities of daily living (14/24, or 58 percent), and nutritional problems (12/18, or 67 percent). On the other hand, emotional problems, problems with spouse, and social/leisure problems were more likely to be major problem areas independent of drinking status. The role played by periods of heavy drinking fell somewhere in the middle for financial problems, housing problems, and family problems. Since the case studies included a higher rate of those admitting to alcohol problems, these results may not apply exactly to the overall clinical population at COPA. Nevertheless, they tend to support a direct relationship between active drinking and problems for some life areas.

Summary

Clients tended to report lower alcohol use and problems than did collateral sources at the time of assessment. In addition, sometimes a clear pattern of the client's alcohol use and problems did not emerge until the client was well into the treatment process. A substantial proportion of clients remained evasive about alcohol use during treatment. The majority of clients had a long history of alcohol abuse. Reported consumption levels were fairly low for clients of addictions treatment and when compared to general population surveys. Since verified alcohol-related problems were high, these apparently low rates of consumption might be attributed to: underrreporting, interactions of alcohol with other drugs, and low tolerance for alcohol due to effects of aging and effects of long-term alcohol abuse. The most frequent alcohol-related problem was the effect of drinking on physical health. Finally, it appeared that some problems in specific life areas (especially cognitive status, nutrition, activities of daily living, and psychiatric problems) were transitory, decreasing during periods of abstinence or low consumption and increasing during heavy drinking periods.

DRUG USE AND PROBLEMS

Drug use in this population consisted primarily of the use of legal medications, as is clearly shown in Table 9. There was only one reported instance of illegal drug use (marijuana). Based on data collected at assessment, the most commonly used drugs were benzodiazepines/antianxiety drugs (38 percent), hypertension medications (18 percent), analgesics (18 percent), antidepressants (16 percent), respiratory-allergy drugs (15 percent), and "other" prescription drugs (21 percent). When drug use was recorded during the treatment process, however, the identified rates of use of certain types of drugs increased dramatically (see Table 10). A much higher use of barbiturates/sleeping pills was identified (from 9 percent of all those assessed to 34 percent of those monitored during the treatment process). Similarly, although only 5.7 percent of those assessed were identified as using antipsychotic medications/major tranquilizers, use of this type of drug was identified for 20 percent of the treatment sample. Combination-use of several different prescription drugs also occurred frequently. Some common combinations were sleeping pills and benzodiazepines (16 people, or 29 percent of cases), antidepressants and benzodiazepines (11 people, or 20 percent), and antidepressants and major tranquilizers (7 people, or 13 percent). Of the 56 clients monitored during treatment, there were only 15 (27 percent) for whom no regular prescription drug use was reported (and some of these may reflect missing data rather than no actual drug use).

TABLE 9. Prescription and Non-prescription Drug Use As Reported at the Time of Assessment

Variable	Proportion consuming each type of drug
Sleeping pills/barbiturates	9.1
Benzodiazepines/antianxiety	37.5
Antidepressants	15.9
Narcotic analgesics (includes 222's, Tylenol 2, 3, 4)	18.1
Anticonvulsants	9.1
Antipsychotics/major tranquilizers	5.7
Respiratory-allergy	14.8
Hypertension medications	18.2
Heart medicine	11.4
Alcohol antagonist	1.1
Other prescription drugs[a]	20.5
Hallucinogens[b]	1.1
Amphetamines	0.0
Solvents	0.0
Volatile nitrates	0.0

Note: n = 88

[a] The category "other" included medications for stomach problems, thyroid, hypoglycemia, gout, muscle spasms, infections, and other physical health problems.

[b] Use of hallucinogens consisted of one person who reported having used marijuana.

These observations suggest relatively high rates of consumption of psychoactive drugs, as well as high rates of consumption of drugs that might interact with alcohol. Drug use was identified as a moderate to extreme problem for 40 to 50 percent of clients at assessment. However, the treatment process data indicated that drug addiction or alcohol-drug interactions were rarely identified as problems by the counselors. Table 11 shows the proportion of clients for whom various drug-use problems were identified on at least one occasion during the treatment process. The most common problem appeared to be poor compliance (taking too much, taking too little, or taking at the wrong time: 48 percent of clients). The next most frequent problems were drugs not having desired effects (18 percent) and drug side effects (18 percent).

Finally, related to substance use but generally not the target of treatment was the use of everyday substances such as tobacco and caffeine. At assessment, 63.7 percent smoked tobacco frequently or daily, 71.4 percent drank coffee frequently or daily, and 53.8 percent drank tea.

TABLE 10. Prescription Drug Use Identified During Assessment and During Treatment Process

Type of drug	Use identified at assessment	Use identified only during treatment	Total number of clients identified as using drug
Sleeping pills/barbiturates	4	15	19 (34%)
Benzodiazepines/antianxiety	20	3	23 (41%)
Antidepressants	9	5	14 (25%)
Analgesics (narcotic and non-narcotic)[a]	14	8	22 (39%)
Anticonvulsants	4	3	7 (13%)
Antipsychotics/major tranquilizers	4	7	11 (20%)
Respiratory-allergy	6	6	12 (21%)
Hypertension medications	8	2	10 (18%)
Heart medicine	6	6	12 (21%)
Other	12	7	19 (34%)

Note: n = 56

[a] Data on whether the analgesic was narcotic or non-narcotic was recorded at assessment, but not recorded as part of data collection during the treatment process.

TABLE 11. Drug Use Problems Identified During Treatment Process

Current drug use problem	Number and proportion of clients who exhibited this problem during the treatment process
Poor compliance with prescribed drug regimen	27 (48%)
Drugs not having desired effect	10 (18%)
Drugs having side effects	10 (18%)
Not taking drugs as prescribed because of alcohol use	7 (13%)
Drug addiction	5 (9%)
Alcohol-drug interactions	5 (9%)
Cost	2 (4%)
Other Problems	6 (11%)

Note: n = 56

Summary

Nearly all drug use by COPA clients involved prescription drugs or over-the-counter medications, with illicit drug use being very rare. Use of psychoactive prescription drugs was high (partly because some clients were referred for drug use problems, not alcohol problems). As with alcohol use, the full extent of psychoactive prescription drug use was usually not apparent at the time of assessment, with much higher use of these drugs becoming known at some time in the treatment process. The most common drug problems identified were poor compliance, drugs not having desired effects, and adverse side effects. Almost two-thirds of COPA clients were current smokers.

PHYSICAL HEALTH

At the time of assessment, the counselor asked clients about their present and past physical health problems. The most common current health problems reported by clients were: musculo-skeletal, particularly arthritis (30 percent); circulatory (20 percent); digestive

(20 percent); and nervous system (18 percent). Other problems included respiratory (14 percent), injuries (14 percent), metabolic diseases (11 percent), genito-urinary (6 percent), and other types of diseases (7 percent). Of the 89 clients for whom there was information on physical health, 37 percent had at least one physical health problem that the counselor considered to be probably related to their alcohol consumption.

Some data were collected about physical health over the course of the treatment process. As previously noted in Table 5, about 80 percent of clients had at least one rating of physical health in the problem range during treatment, and 55 percent had an average rating in the problem range over the course of time in treatment. In addition, the worker reported that physical health problems were at least partly caused by recent alcohol consumption for 63 percent of clients on at least one occasion during treatment.

Summary

Physical health problems were common among COPA clients. Fluctuations in severity of problems often seemed to be related to recent alcohol consumption.

EMOTIONAL/MENTAL HEALTH

The assessment questions did not clearly distinguish among emotional well-being, psychiatric problems, and cognitive/mental functioning. However, some attempt was made to distinguish between emotional health problems and cognitive/mental problems in the data collected as part of client monitoring during treatment. The case studies used anecdotal and other data to further distinguish what appeared to be ongoing psychiatric disorders, from temporary mood fluctuations and from cognitive impairment.

Details of the clients' status at assessment are reported in Tables 12 and 13. The most frequent emotional/mental health problems reported by the clients were loneliness (83 percent), tension/anxiety (81 percent), difficulty sleeping (77 percent), depression (69 percent), and difficulty eating (64 percent). The most common problems observed by the worker at assessment were low energy (57 percent) and unhappy mood state (56 percent).

In addition to the general ratings on emotional and mental health made during the treatment process (previously reported in Table 5), ratings were made of various aspects of emotional or cognitive problems for 38 of the 56 clients in the treatment sample (these ratings were not part of the data collection for the first 12 clients). Table 14 shows the proportion of clients for whom each aspect was rated a problem on at least one occasion during the treatment process. As shown in the table, emotional problems were generally more frequent than cognitive/mental problems. Among the emo-

TABLE 12. Emotional/Mental Health

Type of emotional/mental problem	Proportion who indicated that they had a specific emotional/mental problem at assessment
Loneliness	82.6 (n=86)
Tension/anxiety	81.4 (n=86)
Difficulty sleeping	77.4 (n=84)
Depression	68.6 (n=86)
Difficulty eating	64.3 (n=84)
Trouble concentrating	46.6 (n=73)
Feeling preoccupied/forgetful	41.2 (n=68)
Feeling people are against you	40.0 (n=70)
Feeling inferior to others	36.4 (n=66)
Amnesia/trouble remembering past events	28.8 (n=66)
Feeling aggressive/violent toward others	26.6 (n=64)
Having thoughts of suicide	22.2 (n=63)
Irrational fears/phobias	18.8 (n=69)
Having sexual problems	17.0 (n=53)
Having uncontrollable thoughts/impulses	14.5 (n=55)

tional problems, the most frequently occurring were worry, anxiety, depression, feeling tired or weak, and loneliness. Of the mental/ cognitive problems, the most common were irrationality, poor memory, difficulty concentrating, slowness, and paranoia.

Finally, the data collection during the treatment process included ratings of whether or not the clients' status in a life area at that contact seemed to be caused by recent alcohol consumption. For emotional health, 63 percent of clients were judged on at least one occasion during treatment to have emotional health problems at

TABLE 13. COPA Counselors' Observations of Clients' State During Assessment Interview(s)

Aspect of client's state rated by the counselor	Proportion who had ratings of 1 to 3 on a scale where (1) is poorest and (7) is the best
Energy level (very lethargic to very energetic)	57.3 (n=75)
Mood (very sad to very happy)	56.0 (n=75)
Concentration (very distracted to good concentration)	28.7 (n=87)
Appearance (very unkempt to very well-groomed)	26.4 (n=87)
Memory (great difficulty remembering to excellent memory)	24.1 (n=87)
Speech (great difficulty speaking to fluent and articulate)	16.1 (n=87)
Attitude (very uncooperative to very cooperative)	16.1 (n=87)
Orientation (very disoriented to well-oriented)	13.8 (n=87)
Intoxicated (appeared very intoxicated to appeared completely sober)	11.5 (n=87)

TABLE 14. Emotional or Mental/Cognitive Problems that Emerged During the Treatment Process

Type of problem	Proportion of clients who on at least one occasion had ratings of 4 or 5 on a scale where (1) is not at all and (5) is very much
Emotional:	
worry	79%
anxiety	74%
depression	71%
feeling tired/weak	71%
loneliness	71%
anger/aggression	61%
sleeplessness	61%
grief	55%
frustration	47%
Mental/Cognitive:	
irrationality	47%
poor memory	45%
difficulty concentrating	39%
slowness	37%
paranoia	37%
confusion	29%
impaired speech	29%
disoriented	18%
hallucinations	5%

Note: n = 38. These items were added to the data collection partway through the study and were not available for 18 of the clients who were monitored during the treatment process.

least partly due to recent alcohol consumption. For mental/cognitive problems, 54 percent were judged to have problems at least partly due to recent alcohol consumption.

Summary

The most frequent emotional health problems experienced by COPA clients were loneliness, tension/anxiety, worry/depression, difficulty sleeping and eating, and low energy/feeling tired or weak. The most common mental/cognitive problems observed were irrationality, poor memory, difficulty concentrating, slowness, and paranoia. As with physical health, fluctuations in emotional/mental health were found to be somewhat related to recent level of alcohol consumption.

ACTIVITIES OF DAILY LIVING

The concept of activities of daily living includes care of self and home, as well as ability to manage independently (e.g., cooking, banking, etc.). It is a life area that is frequently used in reference to older people but rarely used in the context of evaluating addictions treatment programs. As was shown in Table 6, activities of daily living were problematic for over half of COPA clients. Some data on basic activities (care of self, clothing, living quarters) over the course of treatment were reported in Table 5. Table 15 shows problems in specific activities at assessment and during the treatment process. Food preparation, shopping, banking, and transportation appeared to be problems for about half of clients at assessment and during the treatment process. On the other hand, although personal hygiene and care of clothing were rated as problems for only about one-quarter of clients at assessment, these emerged as problems at least once during the treatment process, for over half of the clients. Activities of daily living tended to be especially affected by recent alcohol consumption.

Summary

Over half of COPA clients experienced some problems with activities of daily living at least once during treatment. These problems were often associated with recent alcohol use.

SOCIAL/LEISURE

Although isolation and inactivity may be general problems for older persons (especially as physical limitations cause decreases in social contacts and leisure activities), for COPA clients, social and leisure problems seemed to be extremely prevalent. Data were reported on the nature of social contacts for 50 clients at the time of assessment. Of these, 27 percent apparently had no social contacts (outside of agency contacts such as a doctor or visiting nurse). In addition, data were reported on 72 clients about their friendships. Of these, 51 percent reported having problems with friends or having no friends. During the treatment process, the following leisure

TABLE 15. Activities of Daily Living

Type of Activity	Proportion rated poor (1) or fair (2) on a scale from (1) poor to (5) excellent at the time of assessment	Proportion whose most problematic rating fell into problem range during the treatment process
Personal hygiene	22.7 (n=75)	53.6 (n=56)
Care of clothing	24.0 (n=75)	50.0 (n=56)
Care of living quarters	30.6 (n=62)	41.8 (n=55)
Food preparation	60.7 (n=61)	57.1 (n=56)
Use of telephone	34.3 (n=67)	37.5 (n=56)
Ability to conduct shopping	52.4 (n=63)	55.4 (n=56)
Ability to do banking	46.3 (n=54)	50.0 (n=56)
Ability to use methods of transportation	47.0 (n=66)	53.5 (n=56)

problems were reported on at least one occasion: insufficient social contacts (86 percent of clients), insufficient physical activity (73 percent), leisure time not enjoyable (61 percent), little or no activity of any kind (59 percent), and a lack of activities that did not involve alcohol (34 percent). Finally, during the treatment process, 54 percent of clients were rated on at least one occasion as having social/leisure problems at least partly due to recent alcohol consumption.

Summary

COPA clients tended to be extremely isolated, with over half having problems with social relationships, and about two-thirds having problems with use of leisure time. This life area was affected by recent alcohol use, but was also an ongoing problem that tended to continue even when the client was abstinent.

NUTRITION

At assessment, 72 clients rated their own diet and appetite; and for 73 clients, the counselor rated the adequacy of the clients' diets. Ratings of 1 to 3 were considered to be within a problem range (on a scale from (1) very poor to (7) excellent). Among clients, 39 percent rated their appetite in the problem range, and 24 percent rated their diet as a problem; the counselor rated diet as a problem for 41 percent of clients.

During the treatment process, 11 percent of clients were rated on at least one occasion as usually eating too much, and 61 percent were rated as eating too little. In addition, 50 percent were rated on at least one occasion as having nutritional problems that were at least partly caused by recent alcohol consumption.

Summary

Over one-third of clients had nutrition problems, with the most common problem being that the client was eating too little.

ECONOMIC/ACCOMMODATION

Accommodation was rated as a problem by the counselor for over 50 percent of clients at the time of assessment. In addition, economic and accommodation problems ranked high among the life areas of most concern to the clients. At the time of assessment, 43 percent of clients were living alone, and 25 percent were living in temporary accommodations; in terms of satisfaction with accommodations, 53 percent (of the 78 for whom there was information on this question) reported that they found their present living arrangements somewhat or very unsatisfactory.

Types of economic and accommodation problems were monitored during the treatment process and are reported in Table 16. The most common economic problems were: not receiving all income for which they were eligible (25 percent), and having problems due to a very low income (21 percent). The most common accommodation problems were: cohabitants (36 percent), and unsatisfactory physical characteristics of living quarters (e.g., dirty, run-down) (32 percent). Fourteen percent of clients were rated on at least one occasion as having economic problems at least partly due to recent alcohol consumption; 21 percent of clients were rated as having accommodation problems at least partly due to recent alcohol consumption.

Summary

Accommodation and economic problems were fairly frequent among COPA clients, with about half experiencing accommodation problems, and about one-quarter experiencing economic problems. The most common accommodation problems were cohabitants and physical characteristics of living quarters. The most common economic problems were not obtaining all available income, and coping with a very low income.

RELATIONSHIP WITH SPOUSE

Clearly, this life area did not apply to all clients. However, in addition to those who were currently married at the time of treatment, relationship with spouse could be an issue for those who were separated, divorced, or recently widowed. Of the 91 clients assessed, 14 percent were single, 29 percent were living married or common-law, 32 percent were separated or divorced, and 25 percent were widowed.

Data recorded during the treatment process indicated that marital/family discord was a problem on at least one occasion for 18 percent of clients, illness/death of spouse was a problem for 13 percent of clients, alcohol/drug problem of spouse was a problem for 11 percent of clients, and other types of marital/family problems

TABLE 16. Economic and Accommodation Problems that Emerged During the Treatment Process

Type of problem	Proportion of clients who on at least one occasion reported having the problem
Economic:	
May not be receiving all income for which he/she is eligible	25%
Needs help in coping with very low income	21%
Poor money management	18%
Change in economic status	16%
Involved in economic dispute with person or agency	13%
Job search	9%
Other	20%
Accommodation:	
Cohabitants at present accommodation unsatisfactory	36%
Physical characteristics of present accommodation unsatisfactory	32%
Cost of present accommodation unsatisfactory	23%
Cannot live alone	23%
In the process of moving (by own choice)	21%
Geographic location of present accommodation unsatisfactory	20%
Being evicted or forced to move	14%
Other	23%

Note: n=56

were evident for 7 percent of clients. Twenty-seven percent of clients were rated on at least one occasion as having marital problems that were at least partly related to the client's recent alcohol consumption.

Summary

The most common problems related to spouse were marital discord, illness/death of a spouse, and alcohol or drug use by the spouse.

DISCUSSION

Although the clients at COPA are not necessarily representative of all older persons who have substance problems, they are likely a more representative sample of older persons who have alcohol or drug problems than any other treatment sample that has appeared in the scientific literature to date. There are three aspects of the COPA program that increased the likelihood that the sample reflects the population of older persons who have substance problems. First, the nonconfrontational outreach approach resulted in the COPA program reaching a population of older adults who are not typically seen by addictions treatment programs. Second, the data collection procedures used in the COPA evaluation provided the most sensitive measures to date, since data collection occurred both at assessment and during treatment, and involved both self-report and report from others. Graham (1986) argued that the standard approaches to defining alcohol problems among younger people may fail to identify older persons who have alcohol problems. In particular, either criteria used for younger people may not apply to older people (e.g., drinking-related job problems), or cutoffs for criteria are inappropriate (e.g., "safe" levels of consumption for younger people may not be safe for many elderly persons). Therefore, many surveys, while able to sample representatively, cannot accurately identify problems associated with substance abuse among older people because of the lack of a good method for defining and measuring such problems. The inductive and exploratory approach taken in the evaluation at COPA allowed for a very rich description of clients and their problems. Third, the COPA program is located in a multicultural neighborhood of a multicultural city. Although ethnic origin was recorded at intake to COPA, data on ethnicity were not used in the analyses, because the clients came from such a broad range of ethnic backgrounds that global categories were not meaningful. This ethnic diversity of the COPA sample should mean maximal generalizability to North American older people.

In sum, there is reason to believe that the data collected concerning COPA clients, although based exclusively on a treatment sample, can generally further our understanding of the nature of substance problems among the elderly. The following chapter describes some hypotheses or key issues regarding the characteristics of older substance abusers, based on the findings from COPA.

Chapter 7

Problems of Older Alcohol and Drug Abusers

The preceding chapter contained considerable detail on the nature of problems experienced by older alcohol and drug abusers treated at COPA. Because the sample was fairly small, however, these results need to be interpreted cautiously.

The data describing the problems among COPA clients suggest the following conclusions:

- Older alcohol and drug abusers are very likely to have problems with physical health, emotional health, social isolation, and inactivity.
- Other major problem areas for many older substance abusers on at least some occasions were activities of daily living, marital/family relationships, accommodations, prescription drug use, nutrition, and cognitive functioning.
- Some life areas, such as cognitive functioning and activities of daily living, tended to be very sensitive to fluctuations in drinking (e.g., some people experienced problems only during heavy drinking periods).
- Alcohol-related problems may occur for older people at consumption levels that would not usually be problematic for younger people.
- Use of psychoactive prescription drugs is very high among older alcohol abusers.
- Self-reported use of alcohol and psychoactive prescription drugs among older substance abusers is likely to be much lower than actual use.

• Unlike most addictions treatment populations, older substance abusers have a very low rate of illicit drug use.

These conclusions are discussed in greater detail in the following sections.

HIGH RATE OF PROBLEMS WITH PHYSICAL HEALTH, EMOTIONAL HEALTH, SOCIAL ISOLATION, AND INACTIVITY

As previously shown in Table 6, over three-quarters of COPA clients were found to have problems in the areas of physical health, emotional health, isolation, and use of leisure time (i.e., inactivity). A later study of case management at COPA (Graham, Birchmore Timney, & White-Campbell, 1990) replicated these findings exactly, with these areas (and no other areas) also rated problematic for 75 percent or more of COPA clients in the later study.

Physical Health

According to data collected at COPA, physical health problems were observed on at least one occasion for 75 percent of the treatment sample. In addition, physical health was the third highest area of concern by clients at the time of assessment, with 45 percent rating this an area of moderate to extreme worry. This rate of physical health problems can be compared to the results from a 1987 survey of senior citizen apartments in Toronto by Adlaf, Smart, and Jansen (1989), where 11 percent of respondents rated themselves in poor overall health, 18 percent reported that their health problems impeded their activities a great deal, and 29 percent reported a serious illness in the past 12 months. Other general population surveys have also shown lower rates of physical health problems than observed at COPA. In a 1989 Canadian survey,[1] (Health and Welfare Canada, 1990) 25 percent of people aged 65 and over reported that their health was fair to poor, and the remaining 75

---

1. Figures were calculated using the publicly available dataset of this survey.

percent reported their health to be good, very good, or excellent. In a random sample household survey in St. John's, Newfoundland (Segovia, Bartlett, & Edwards, 1989), about 30 percent of respondents aged 65 and over reported that their health was poor or fair, 30 to 40 percent reported some or much worry about their health, and 11 percent reported being not too satisfied or not at all satisfied about their physical condition. Finally, these results are consistent with conclusions drawn from existing literature (previously presented in Table 3) that older alcohol abusers are likely to have physical health problems.

Since estimates of prevalence of physical health problems seem to vary according to how this construct is defined and measured, it is difficult to compare numbers from COPA without measuring physical health status *in exactly the same way* in a sample of older people who do not have alcohol or drug problems. Nevertheless, the data suggest that physical health is considerably more problematic for older persons who have alcohol or drug problems than for older people generally.

Emotional Problems

Among COPA clients in the treatment sample, 37 percent expressed a moderate to extreme worry about emotional/mental health problems, and 88 percent were rated by the COPA counselor as having a moderate to extreme need for assistance in the area of emotional/mental health. In addition, 83 percent of all COPA clients assessed indicated loneliness, 81 percent tension/anxiety, 77 percent difficulty sleeping, and 69 percent depression. By contrast, in the Toronto survey (Adlaf, Smart, & Jansen, 1989), 54 percent of respondents reported that these were the best years of their lives, 10 percent reported feeling very lonely, and 8 percent reported feeling depressed. In the St. John's survey (Segovia, Bartlett, & Edwards, 1989), about 11 percent of respondents aged 65 and over reported emotional status as fair or poor, and 6 percent reported that they were not too happy or were unhappy. A recent study of persons aged 65 and over in London, England (Lindesay, Briggs, & Murphy, 1989) found one-month prevalence rates for depression to be 13.5 percent, anxiety disorder 3.7 percent, and phobic disorders 10 percent.

As with physical health status, when problems are defined and measured differently, exact comparisons are not possible. However, even these rough comparisons suggest that COPA clients are highly distressed in terms of emotional health. This may be partly a factor of COPA data being drawn from a treatment sample, most of whom entered treatment because their problems came to the attention of workers in health and social service agencies. It is possible that those who have alcohol or drug problems, but do not come to the attention of typical referral sources for COPA, are less likely to have emotional problems. On the other hand, depression and anxiety tend to characterize substance abusing populations of all ages (Graham & Ekdahl, 1986); therefore, it might be assumed that these data reflect a real relationship between emotional problems and substance abuse among the elderly. These results are generally consistent with the high rate of mental/emotional health problems among older alcohol abusers concluded from previous studies (see Table 3).

Social Isolation and Inactivity

As was apparent in Table 6, adequacy of social/leisure activity was an area of great discrepancy between the extent of the problem as perceived by the counselors and the extent that this life area was of concern to clients. About one-quarter of clients rated social or leisure problems as a moderate to extreme worry; whereas for about three-quarters of clients, the COPA counselor rated social/leisure problems as moderate to extreme. Therefore, in comparing the results from COPA to data on social leisure problems among older people generally, the interpretation of the extent of problems among COPA clients depends on whether it is measured by the client's worry or the counselor's rating. However, other data collected from self-report of COPA clients suggest that the lack of worry or concern expressed may not be indicative of a lack of problems. Of clients who participated in treatment at COPA, 32 clients provided data on social interactions. Of these, 22 percent had no social contacts or contacts only with agency workers, while 60 percent reported that they had at least one close friend. Of the 39 who provided information about their social relationships, 41 percent reported that they had problems with friends or had no friends. In addition, 80 percent of all those assessed complained of loneliness. During the treatment process, 86 percent of clients were rated by the counselor as having insufficient social contacts, and 59 percent were rated as having little or no social activities of any kind.

There are no exactly comparable data available on social and leisure activities of older people who do not have substance problems. Among the sample survey of Adlaf, Smart, and Jansen (1989), 9 percent reported feeling lonely often, 27 percent reported not having enough friends, and 20 percent reported not having enough to do to keep busy. Eighty-seven percent of their sample reported having someone to confide in, 85 percent reported having someone to depend on if ill, 43 percent participated in recreational activities often, 79 percent reported doing volunteer work, and 26 percent reported socializing with friends often. Among the sample of elderly (persons aged 65 and over) in Newfoundland (Segovia, Bartlett, & Edwards, 1989), only 5 percent of men and 1 percent of women reported having no social contact with either close friends or close family. In a Canadian national survey (see Health and Welfare Canada, 1990), respondents were asked how supportive or helpful family and friends were when the respondent had needed help over the previous 12 months (very helpful, helpful, somewhat helpful, not helpful); only 4 percent of respondents aged 65 and older reported that family and friends were not helpful, with an additional 6 percent reporting that they were somewhat helpful.

Consistent with the conclusions of previous studies of older alcohol abusers (shown in Table 3), COPA clients had fewer satisfying social relationships and less social/activities than other samples of non-substance-abusing older people. However, social/leisure needs are highly variable and there are no standard criteria for how many friends or social activities a person *should* have. Nevertheless, the case studies indicated that alcohol abuse was often part of a lifestyle of social isolation and inactivity, and part of the COPA approach was to help clients reduce drinking by engaging in satisfying social/ leisure activities that did not involve alcohol use. In sum, although it seems that alcohol abuse is part of a pattern of behavior involving social/leisure problems, research is required to understand the relationship between substance problems and social/leisure problems.

MODERATE TO HIGH PROBLEMS
AMONG OLDER SUBSTANCE ABUSERS
IN THE AREAS OF ACTIVITIES OF DAILY LIVING,
MARITAL/FAMILY RELATIONSHIPS, ACCOMMODATION,
PRESCRIPTION DRUG USE, NUTRITION,
AND COGNITIVE FUNCTIONING

Some life areas found to be moderately problematic among COPA clients relate to being older, and typically have not been examined in studies of younger substance abusers. In particular, while most studies of older people include measures of activities of daily living, nutrition, and sometimes cognitive functioning, these issues are rarely considered for younger people, including younger substance abusers. Similarly, use of prescription drugs tends to be paid little attention, if at all, in studies of younger people. For the older person, however, these areas (including marital/family relationships) are the key areas in the person's maintenance of independent living. The high rates of problems in these areas (50 percent or more of COPA clients) among older alcohol abusers, make this group especially vulnerable to institutionalization.

Since activities of daily living, cognitive functioning, and high prescription drug use are seen to be general problems of aging, not all of these problems can be attributable to alcohol use. Sometimes long-term alcohol use can be identified as a factor in the development of these types of problems (e.g., Korsakoff's syndrome, or alcohol-related dementia). Sometimes problems seem to be caused by nondrinking events in the person's life (e.g., arthritis affecting ability to deal with activities of daily living). Usually, however, alcohol use aggravates existing problems, and reducing use could result in a considerable reduction in the problem severity, thus allowing the person to maintain independence.

Similarly, accommodation problems cannot always be attributed to alcohol abuse. Accommodation problems were high among COPA clients (over 50 percent). Without an appropriate comparison group, however, it is difficult to speculate on the extent to which these problems were due to (1) consequences of long-term substance abuse, (2) consequences of recent substance abuse, (3) problems generally associated with housing for the elderly, (4) problems generally associated with the high cost of housing in Toronto, and (5) the tendency for housing problems to be the crisis that led to the client being referred to COPA. As with accommodation, a number of COPA clients were experiencing economic hardship; however, the data did not provide a means of teasing out the role played by alcohol. Since the majority of COPA clients were not of employable status (i.e., were either retired or receiving disability benefits), most economic problems seemed to be related to living on a very low income or not being aware of other sources of income for which they were eligible. Although long-term substance abuse may have led to the person being poor in old age, there was no strong evidence that current substance abuse was causing increased economic problems for many clients.

Marital and family problems are generally related to substance abuse regardless of age. With COPA clients, breaks with family were often of long duration. Thus, a common family problem was having no contact with family (particularly children). Other problems included marital/family conflict and drinking by family members.

The literature on these life areas (previously summarized in Table 3) did not indicate consistent support for problems in these life areas among older substance abusers, although at least some studies found more cognitive problems, more tranquilizer use, high incidence of self-neglect, and frequent moves among older substance abusers.

LIFE AREAS MOST AFFECTED BY VARIATIONS IN ALCOHOL USE

Many life areas were affected by whether or not the client was in an abstinent/light drinking period or a heavy drinking period. The areas especially affected seemed to be: physical health, emotional health, activities of daily living, and cognitive functioning. The latter two are of particular interest, since for some clients, problems occurred in these areas *only* during heavy drinking periods. For these clients, these areas tended to be reliable markers that the client was drinking.

Activities of Daily Living

The data from the COPA program indicated *high variability* in problems of care of self and living quarters. In the case study analyses, 67 percent of cases were identified as having problems with self-care, but of these, over half had these problems *only* during periods of heavy drinking. The immediate relationship between alcohol use and self-care was also evident from the quantitative analyses of client contact data where a significant relationship was found between problem drinking status at each contact and problems in personal hygiene (these analyses are presented in more detail in Chapter 9, Table 22). These findings would suggest that variability in care of self and living quarters among older people may be indicative of binging or intermittent heavy use of drugs or alcohol. This relationship between alcohol use and poor self-care among older people has been supported in a description of two case studies of Senile Squalor Syndrome (Kafetz & Cox, 1982).

Cognitive Functioning

The research at COPA did not set out specifically to examine cognitive impairment. Although the Mini Mental Status Exam (Folstein, Folstein, & McHugh, 1975) was used in some cases for screening at assessment, in general, the clinical staff preferred to keep contacts friendly and informal without subjecting the client to extensive formal testing. Severe cases were referred to geriatric specialists for assessment. Even without formal testing, however, it became apparent that cognitive impairment was a consequence of alcohol consumption for some COPA clients.

The relationship between long-term alcohol abuse and cognitive deterioration is well known, as is the relationship between aging and increased cognitive deficits. It might be expected, therefore, that a sample of elderly alcohol abusers would demonstrate a high rate of cognitive impairment. In fact, about 25 percent of the COPA treatment sample showed cognitive problems on an ongoing basis. However, there was also very high variability on the ratings of cognitive status, with 63 percent rated as having problems on at least one occasion during treatment, *but* 96 percent rated as good to ideal (!) on at least one occasion.

Several issues emerged from studying this sample. First, for some clients who never abstained from alcohol use, it was difficult to discriminate cognitive problems due to recent alcohol consumption from impairment that existed regardless of consumption. Second, for a number of clients, cognitive functioning and alcohol use covaried almost perfectly: during drinking phases, a client could be cognitively impaired to the point of confusion and lack of adequate self-care; during nondrinking periods, the same client might exhibit almost complete recovery from cognitive problems. It is tempting to speculate that the causal relationship was that alcohol use led to cognitive problems. There were cases, however, where it appeared that a period of more severe cognitive problems may have led to either ending a period of abstinence or increasing moderate alcohol consumption above moderate levels. Since even among clients who maintained sobriety there was considerable variability in cognitive impairment, it is plausible that periods of increased cognitive impairment may weaken a conscious resolve not to drink. Finally, there was a handful of clients who, soon after referral to COPA, showed a very rapid decline in cognitive status, ending in institutionalization. Given the age of the sample, that this would happen to a small proportion of clients is not surprising. What was surprising, however, was that major problems related to cognitive status were often not apparent at the time of assessment or during the initial contacts with the COPA counselor.

In sum, a great deal more needs to be known about the relationship between cognitive problems and alcohol abuse among older persons. This is an important practical concern because cognitive problems may necessitate institutionalization. There may need to be special methods for helping older people avoid "slips" into heavy drinking during periods when they are not thinking very clearly. It may also be important for total abstinence to be strongly encouraged when cognitive problems are implicated.

ALCOHOL-RELATED PROBLEMS ASSOCIATED WITH RELATIVELY LOW LEVELS OF CONSUMPTION

Although there was some doubt about the accuracy of self-report by clients at COPA, nevertheless, there seemed to be at least some cases where problems were associated with validated low levels of consumption. This is consistent with the finding by Blazer et al. (1984) that older alcoholics tend to report lower maximum alcohol consumption than younger alcoholics. This may be a function of older people being especially vulnerable to the effects of alcohol because of lower tolerance (due to effects of physical aging and/or damage to the body from previous substance abuse, or because of other factors of aging such as higher prescription drug use). However, nearly all surveys that use consumption data to estimate the rate of problem use (e.g., Hilton, 1988) use the same cutoffs regardless of age. The finding of major problems exhibited by COPA clients with relatively low rates of consumption suggests that care needs to be taken in defining problem levels for different segments of the population. Even among older people (i.e., 65 and over), there may be variability in problem levels, with the young-old being more able than the old-old to tolerate moderate to high levels of consumption.

Table 17 shows quantity and frequency of reported drinking by COPA clients compared to results from the same type of questions asked of a Canadian National Survey (see Health and Welfare Canada, 1990), a general Ontario survey (Smart & Adlaf, 1987) and a survey of Toronto older people living in senior citizens' apartments (Adlaf, Smart, & Jansen, 1989). As shown in this table, COPA clients were more likely to report daily drinking than were any of the other samples. On the other hand, while only 33 percent of COPA clients reported a maximum consumption of five or more drinks in a single sitting, 40 percent of Canadian adults reported this level, and over 50 percent of Ontario adults (30 percent of Ontario adults aged 50 and over) reported this level. The respondents from seniors' apartments reported a low rate of ever drinking five or more drinks (7 percent), possibly reflecting the inclusion of a large proportion of very elderly in the sample (average age of respondents from seniors' apartments was 74, while the average age of COPA clients was around 64). The rate of high-volume drinking was also very low for those aged 65 and over in the Canadian National Survey. From other information collected at COPA, the relatively low rate of high-volume drinking was attributable to two factors: (1) underreporting, and (2) lower tolerance due to effects of

TABLE 17. Drinking and Drug Use Reported by Clients Who Received Treatment at COPA Compared to Reported Alcohol and Drug Use by Adults Aged 18 Years and Over in a Canadian National Survey[a], an Ontario Survey[b], and Compared to Use Reported by Respondents in a Toronto Survey of Senior Citizen Apartments[c]

		Canadian survey		Ontario survey		Residents of senior citizens apartments in Toronto aged 60 and over
	COPA clients	All adults in survey[a]	Adults aged 65 and over in survey[a]	All adults in survey[b]	Adults aged 50 and over in survey[b]	
Daily drinking	43%[d,e]	5%	10%	12%	17%	11%
Ever drinking 5 or more drinks at a single sitting	33%[d,f]	38%	10%	55%	29%	7%
Minor tranquilizers	40%[d]	3%	5%	7%	11%[g]	13%
Sleeping pills	29%[d]	4%	11%	9%[g]	11%[g]	23%

[a] Canadian National Alcohol and Drug Survey (1989) - taken from publicly available database (see Health and Welfare Canada, 1990).
[b] Smart, R. G., & Adlaf, E. M. (1987). Alcohol and Other Drug Use Among Ontario Adults 1977-1987. Toronto: Addiction Research Foundation.
[c] Adlaf, E. M., Smart, R. G., & Jansen, V. A. (1989). Alcohol Use, Drug Use and Well-Being Among a Sample of Older Adults in Toronto: Preliminary Report. Toronto: Addiction Research Foundation.
[d] n=48, excludes COPA clients who were seen for drug problems only (i.e., includes those identified as having only alcohol problems or both alcohol and drug problems).
[e] 9 missing cases
[f] 19 missing cases
[g] Percentage using drugs at least once in past 12 months.

129

aging, effects of long-term alcohol use, or interactions with concurrent drug use.

As shown in Table 17, COPA clients who were identified as having alcohol problems also tended to be heavier users of psychoactive prescription drugs (namely, minor tranquilizers and sleeping pills) than all aged adults, and older adults. Drug use by COPA clients was also substantially higher than use reported by the elderly in a number of Canadian and American surveys cited by McKim and Mishara (1987), where combined use of tranquilizers and/or hypnotics ranged from 2.8 percent to 15.6 percent. These findings are consistent with high rates of multiple drug use common among nonelderly addictions treatment samples. The high use of psychoactive prescription drugs among COPA clients who were alcohol abusers suggests that programs treating elderly persons who have alcohol problems need to be alert to potential concurrent drug problems. In addition, physicians need to be more careful about obtaining valid estimates of alcohol use among their elderly patients before prescribing drugs that might interact or have a synergistic effect with alcohol.

UNDERREPORTING OF ALCOHOL AND DRUG USE BY OLDER PEOPLE

As previously shown in Table 7, levels of alcohol use and problems were much lower when based on self-report than when levels were assessed using collateral sources. This finding was not unexpected, since those unwilling to admit to heavy or problem use were particularly targeted by the program. Nevertheless, these results suggest that when primary caregivers such as physicians and nurses suspect that alcohol abuse may be implicated in a patient's health problems, self-report may not be a reliable method of assessing this area. The safest approach for those delivering primary care would seem to be to be caution where alcohol abuse is suspected (even if not confirmed). This caution would especially apply to the prescribing of psychoactive drugs.

COPA clients also appeared to underreport use of prescription drugs (particularly sleeping pills and major tranquilizers) at the time of assessment. These results *were* surprising, and suggest that obtaining accurate prescription drug use data may not be as straight-forward as usually believed.

LOW RATE OF ILLICIT DRUG USE
AMONG OLDER PEOPLE

The only illicit drug use reported by COPA clients was by one person who occasionally smoked marijuana. Surveys generally support the conclusion of a low rate of illicit drug use among the elderly (McKim & Mishara, 1987). Insofar as drug-using behaviors and culture are different for illicit drugs, the existing low use of illicit drugs among older people would support the position that the treatment or counseling needs of older substance abusers are likely to be different than the needs of younger alcohol and drug abusers (who are much more likely to be part of an illicit drug using culture).

SUMMARY

In summary, the major problem areas among older substance abusers are physical health, emotional health, social isolation, and inactivity. In addition, data from COPA indicate that over half of older substance abusers are also likely to experience problems in activities of daily living, marital/family relationships, accommodations, prescription drug use, nutrition, and cognitive functioning. Some life areas such as activities of daily living and cognitive functioning seem to be particularly affected by high levels of alcohol use. Intermittent problems in these areas may well indicate an alcohol problem. Underreporting of alcohol and drug use was high among COPA clients. However, there seemed to be at least some evidence that older people experience problems at lower levels of consumption than would ordinarily affect younger people. Finally, compared to the general population of older persons, older alcohol abusers are more likely to use psychoactive prescription drugs; compared to younger alcohol abusers, older abusers are much less likely to use illicit drugs.

Chapter 8

Measuring Client Outcomes

A primary goal of the present research was to examine not only the nature of substance abuse among the elderly, but also the effects of treatment. In particular, the research was intended to address the questions: What proportion of clients appeared to benefit from the program? In what ways (life areas) did they exhibit improvement? And, what were the client and other factors associated with improvement? In order to address these questions, it was necessary to develop a new approach to assessing client outcomes. For various reasons (including lack of data at assessment), the usual pretest/posttest approach to evaluation was inappropriate. In addition, since other life areas were specifically targeted for treatment, outcome measures needed to include assessment in these other life areas as well. Finally, outcome measures in other life areas were needed to evaluate the relationship between reduced substance abuse and reduced problems in other life areas. Accordingly, the standard measure of program success for an addictions treatment program (i.e., reduced substance abuse) was relevant to the present research, but problematic because of the nature of the program. In addition, outcome measures in life areas other than substance abuse were perceived to be important measures in their own right.

The major source of outcome information was the monitoring data collected about each client throughout treatment. During the research project, however, two other sources of outcome data were developed: a clinical rating of overall status at discharge (using a discharge form developed by the program staff); and subjective ratings of overall improvement made by the principal investigator for those clients included in the case studies. While it was intended that the outcome measures for quantitative analyses be based on the monitoring data (which provided detailed information about the changes in client status during treatment), the other two sources of outcome information provided an opportunity for assessing the validity of the outcomes from monitoring. The following two sections describe first the calculations of outcome ratings in specific life areas, and then the strategy for assigning overall outcome ratings to clients (including a discussion of the validity of the overall outcome ratings). Subsequently, Chapter 9 will describe client, program, and other factors related to positive outcomes.

OUTCOME MEASURES FOR EACH LIFE AREA BASED ON MONITORING DATA

Monitoring involved recording the client's status in each life area at every contact, with more detail provided when the life area was problematic (see Appendix A, Client Contact Record). The life area variables on which outcome measures were calculated included the following: alcohol problems and frequency of drinking during the week preceding each contact, drug use status, physical health, emotional health, mental/cognitive health, personal hygiene, care of clothing, care of living quarters, adequacy of diet, appetite, social contacts, leisure activities, economic status, accommodation status, and relationship with spouse.

Two different types of outcome scores were calculated initially: a trend score, and a change score. The Pearson correlation coefficient was chosen as a quantitative measure of the trend of the client's status in each life area over time in treatment. The outcome measure which was developed to measure the trend of change in each life area consisted of the average of two correlations calculated for each client separately: (1) the correlation between client status and days in treatment, and (2) the correlation between client status and number of treatment contacts. These correlations were calculated only for clients for whom there were at least five data points on that variable (i.e, at least five contacts where the client's status in that life area was recorded).

In addition, a change score for each variable was calculated. This score consisted of the difference between the average of the last two scores and the average of the first two scores on each life area variable. The pre-post approach to calculating a change score is the most conventional approach to evaluating client outcomes; that is, it directly examines whether the client was better off at the end of treatment than he or she had been at the beginning. Using the first and last contacts provided a procedure that could be used across all clients (whether there were five contacts or 95 contacts). By averaging the scores rather than taking only the single first and last scores, the reliability of these scores was increased, since the variability associated with use of a single score was reduced. However, the pre-post score was not used as a single outcome measure in the present study because of problems with pre-post measurement when usedwith the COPA approach and with older people generally. In fact, both methods of measuring outcomes had deficiencies. The correlations could identify only linear trends (and were unstable where the number of data points was small). On the other hand, the change scores reflected the client's status (which may be quite variable) at only two periods during treatment (beginning and end), and could not utilize process information relating to overall progress or deterioration of the client. Therefore, the two different approaches to measuring outcomes in particular life areas were combined to produce a single outcome rating for each life area in order to improve the rating's robustness and validity.

Before combining the two measures, each type of measure was recoded into three global categories: Improved, Unchanged, or Worse. For correlation scores, the range of scores from $r = -.19$ to $r = .19$ was rated Unchanged, $r = .20$ or larger was rated Improved, and $r = -.20$ or less was rated Worse. For difference scores (based on 3-point, 4-point, and 5-point scales), a change score of 1 or more was rated Improved, a score of .9 to $-.9$ was rated Unchanged, and a score of -1 or less was rated Worse. For the health measures (based on a 0-100 scale), a change score of 10 or more was rated Improved, 9 to -9 as Unchanged, and -10 or less as Worse.

To compare the two measures, the three categories based on the correlations were cross-tabulated with the three categories derived from the difference scores for each variable. Ratings were considered consistent if both were categorized Improved, both were categorized Worse, or both were categorized Unchanged. Ratings were also considered "consistent" where one was categorized Unchanged and the other either Worse or Improved. Inconsistent cases were defined as those where one rating was categorized Worse and the other Improved. Using these definitions, of the 16 outcome variables compared for the 56 cases, only two instances of inconsistency were identified–both for the variable measuring emotional health. To resolve these inconsistencies, the case files were examined and it was concluded that both cases should be rated as Unchanged on this variable.

In order to combine the two scores (the correlation and the change score) into one final outcome measure for each life area variable, the following procedures were used:

1. Missing data. As described previously, correlations were calculated only where there existed at least five data points on the variable. For the change scores, the score was based on the difference between the average of the first two scores and the last two scores. If one of the final scores or one of the first scores was missing, the change score was calculated based on the single non-missing score. If both initial scores or both final scores were missing, no change score could be calculated (i.e., the change score on that variable for that client was defined as Missing). In addition, if the final two scores were missing, the correlation change score was also defined as Missing. Thus, some information concerning status on the final contacts had to be available in order for either of the change scores to be defined as non-missing.

2. Direction of change. If *either* the correlation change score *or* the difference change score was categorized Improved, the summary rating was defined as Improved (i.e., the summary rating might be Improved even though one of the scores was rated Unchanged or defined as Missing). Similarly, the summary rating was defined as Deteriorated if either the correlation score or the difference score was categorized Worse. The summary variable was rated Unchanged if both change scores were categorized Unchanged, or one was Unchanged and one was Missing.

3. Final change scores incorporating the client's initial status. While it was important that change scores be sensitive to small, but important, changes in client status, there were certain types of changes that were not of clinical or research interest. In particular, changes that occurred within a *non-problem range* of a particular life area variable were not of relevance to the study. For example, on physical health, a rating between 80 to 100 was defined as Good to Ideal. Within this range, a person might receive a rating of 85 on the first contact and 95 on the final contact and be defined as Improved; alternatively, the person might receive a score of 95 on the first contact and 85 on the final contact and be defined as Deteriorated. However, although these scores may reflect real changes in the person's well-being, changes in life areas that are never perceived to be problematic are not of interest for the present study. Therefore, the outcome scores on each variable were recoded to incorporate data regarding whether or not an area was in the problem range at assessment, at initial contacts, or at final contacts. The scores were redefined as follows:

Improved (a score of 1). This category was used when (1) the summary change score was defined as Improved; and (2) the person began at COPA with either an assessment rating in the problem range for that life area, or had initial contact scores in the problem range;

Unchanged (a score of 0). A variable was rated Unchanged when (1) the summary change score was defined as Unchanged, or (2) the summary change score was defined as Improved, but the person did not begin treatment with a score in the problem range for that life area; or (3) the summary change score was defined as Deteriorated, but the person neither began nor ended treatment with a score in the problem range for that life area.

Deteriorated (a score of –1). This rating was used when (1) the person received a summary change score of Deteriorated; and (2) the person either began or ended treatment with a score in the problem range for that area.

DEVELOPMENT OF OVERALL OUTCOME SCORES

It was decided at the beginning of the project that "success" would not be defined solely on the basis of a change in alcohol or drug consumption, since the program was committed to a more holistic approach to helping persons who had substance problems. To this end, while it was important to identify particular life areas that improved in treatment, it was also considered useful to identify cases that seemed to improve overall (i.e., the overall "success rate" of the program).

As a first step toward defining overall success, a total score was computed based on the sum of the scores in each life area (described in the preceding section). These computed scores were then compared to other outcome information to assess the validity of the computed scores, and to revise the method of computing scores, as appropriate.

The Three Sources of Outcome Ratings

For 24 clients, there were three different sources of outcome information. These sources included (1) overall change as measured using change scores from the client monitoring data, (2) clinical ratings of status at discharge as reported by the counselor, and (3) global ratings of change in status during treatment made by the principal investigator on the basis of the case study data.

Outcome Scores Based on Monitoring

The use of monitoring data to produce outcome measures was chosen for the study for a number of reasons. First, monitoring provided a quantitative and fairly objective method of assessing the changes made by the clients during treatment. Second, this method provided measures of change in each life area so that it would be possible to identify exactly where improvements occurred. Finally, the rating of overall improvement could be done without bias, using some computational method for combining status scores in each life area.

There appears to be no previous research in which outcome scores were developed on the basis of monitoring information where the number of client contacts, the nature of problems, and the types of interventions varied from client to client to the extent that occurred among clients in the COPA program. Methods developed from research on clinical trials could not be used directly in the present study because each client received a unique set of interventions over an open-ended time interval. Therefore, a new procedure for calculating improvement scores had to be developed for the present study. As described in the preceding section, this procedure consisted of defining the improvement score for each life area as either: (1) Improved, (0) Unchanged or (-1) Deteriorated. From these ratings, the overall outcome score was computed by summing the improvement scores for each client across 12 life areas. This process included combining or excluding certain measures; namely, the two alcohol ratings were combined for one score; and care of clothing, care of living quarters, and rating of appetite were excluded in the overall score, as these were somewhat redundant with two other variables that were included (personal hygiene and adequacy of diet). If the total of this summing was positive, the case was defined as improved overall (e.g., if a person Improved in two life areas, Deteriorated in one area, and was Unchanged in the remaining life areas, the net change score for that client was "Improved"). Scores that summed to 0 were classified as Unchanged overall, and minus scores were considered Deteriorated. For the 24 cases used in the present analyses, this process resulted in 18 cases classified as Improved, two cases classified as Unchanged, and four cases classified as Deteriorated. Since this approach was new, these results were compared to other available information on outcomes to provide some validation of the approach.

Clinical Outcome Ratings

Outcome ratings made by counselors are generally suspected of being positively biased. The counselor is not indifferent to the outcome of the client whom he or she has counseled–that is, in most cases the counselor wants to believe that the person has improved. Furthermore, recollection of pretreatment status (as a comparison point) may be vague, and this may add further error to assessment of the changes made by the client. In the discharge form developed by the counselors for their own use, the categories used for describing the client's status at discharge contained more positive than negative categories, potentially reflecting additional positive bias. These categories included: Successfully Maintained, Substantial Improvement, Moderate Improvement, Little-or-No-Improvement, and Deteriorated. The other technical problem that made clear interpretation of the scale difficult was that although Successfully Maintained was considered to be the optimum rating, it was technically possible that a person who was Successfully Maintained might have improved only slightly (and so not to have qualified for the lesser rating of Substantial Improvement). Thus, the issue of extent of improvement was somewhat confused in the ratings with stability of improvement. Nevertheless, the ratings from this scale provide a useful measure of the clinician's perspective regarding the client's outcome. Overall, the clinical ratings indicated mostly positive outcomes for these 24 cases, with 15 rated Successfully Maintained, five rated Substantial Improvement, three rated Moderate Improvement, and one rated Little-or-No-Improvement.

Global Outcome Ratings Made on the Basis of Case Studies

The global ratings made in the context of the case studies were somewhat comparable to the ratings made by the counselors at discharge, in that they consisted of subjective ratings made on the basis of one person's overall impression of the case. Presumably, the ratings were somewhat less positively biased since they were made by the principal investigator rather than the case worker (although it is probably unrealistic to believe that a researcher can work with a program for several years and remain totally impartial about the results of the program!). A symmetric scale was used for this process, resulting in the following: seven cases were rated Very Improved, 11 Somewhat Improved, five cases were rated Unchanged or Uncertain whether real change had occurred, one case was rated Somewhat Worse, and no cases were rated Much Worse.

Comparison of Outcome Ratings

Comparing the three methods, the counselor rated 23 of the 24 clients Improved-to-Some-Extent, the principal investigator rated 18 cases Improved, and the monitoring method identified 18 cases as Improved. Of the 24 cases, 13 were rated Improved by all three sources; five cases were rated Improved by the counselor and the principal investigator (but these ratings were not supported by the monitoring data); four cases were rated Improved by the case worker and supported by the monitoring data (but not rated Improved by the investigator); one case was rated Improved only by the counselor; and one case was assessed as Improved only on the basis of the monitoring data.

Interpreting Discrepancies in Comparing Outcome Ratings

The detailed case studies made it possible to examine and interpret discrepancies that emerged in comparing outcome ratings from the three methods. One major source of discrepancy was *the relative importance placed on information regarding drinking status*. In calculating the overall *monitoring* score, change in drinking status was weighted equally with change scores from the other 11 life areas. However, improvements in drinking status were accorded special status in the counselor's ratings and by the principal investigator in making ratings on the case studies. In two of the five cases where the counselor and the investigator judged that the clients had improved but the monitoring information showed no change or deterioration, the person had reduced his or her drinking or had become abstinent but had deteriorated in a number or other life areas. Since the program was aimed at drinking status, these two cases were rated as successes by the counselor and the investigator. However, when drinking status was treated as one of a number of life areas, the cases emerged overall as not improved.

Another source of discrepancy in the ratings is the *use by the counselor and the investigator of pretreatment information or other sources of information* which were not included in the client monitoring. For example, if a person became abstinent at entry into COPA and then resumed frequent drinking, this emerged in the monitoring data as deterioration in the area of alcohol consumption. However, if the later drinking appeared to be much less than the pretreatment levels were known to be, the counselor and the investigator rated this person as "improved" (based on comparison to data in the client's file about pretreatment status). Another instance of discrepancy occurred when follow-up information was available and described in the case notes, but was not recorded as part of monitoring because the counselor was not having direct contact with the client. In this instance, the case notes described information from other sources which indicated that the client was drinking heavily and doing poorly (thus leading to negative ratings by the

COPA counselor and the investigator); however, this information was not reported on the monitoring forms (thus resulting in a neutral or positive outcome on the basis of the monitoring data).

One source of discrepancy between the principal investigator's ratings and outcome ratings by the counselor related to the *judgment of stability of change for clients who had a pattern of binging and abstinence*. In both cases where discrepancies occurred, the clients were discharged during a period of abstinence. The case worker rated them as showing successful maintenance, and the monitoring data showed overall improvement. However, the investigator rated these cases "no change or uncertain" because the evidence did not seem strong that the cycle of binging had been resolved. Both clients had been on a binge within the four months prior to discharge, and both had a history of periods of abstinence in between binges. In fact, the follow-up data suggested that both cases continued to engage in binge drinking to some extent (although for one of the cases, these periods of heavy drinking did not appear to be causing problems at follow-up).

Apparent positive bias in subjective ratings seemed to account for several discrepancies. In one case, the person died while in treatment; near the end, this person was drinking heavily and exhibiting deterioration in other areas. However, the person initially had been very highly motivated and had shown good progress. When the client's terminal illness was diagnosed, the client resumed drinking and all life areas gradually deteriorated until the client died. Both the investigator and the counselor chose to believe that the initial progress would have been maintained had the terminal illness not intervened and, therefore, rated this person improved (despite obvious deterioration!). In another instance, the client had made gains, but had resumed heavy drinking by the time she dropped out of treatment. While the counselor rated her as improved (presumably on the basis of early gains), the investigator rated her as deteriorated (since she seemed to have resumed problem drinking), and the monitoring data showed her status to be unchanged in all areas.

Marginal cases created another source of apparent discrepancy. In two cases, the investigator rated the client as the same (or uncertain whether change had occurred), and the counselor rated the client as moderately improved (the lowest improvement category); however, the monitoring data indicated fairly consistent improvement in a number of categories. For one client, problems with personal relationships, health, and so on seemed to be unresolved at the time that her boyfriend forced her to withdraw from COPA. However, early in treatment, she had experienced some very severe crises. Since her subsequent crises were less severe, the improvement shown by the monitoring (and recognized by the counselor) was probably accurate. For the other marginal case, the improved status (from both the counselor and the monitoring) seemed to be based largely on the improvement noted only on the final visit, where the client reported that he had reduced his drinking (a statement not corroborated by his wife). The text of the case notes, however, did not indicate that the client was improved, especially since he was being discharged for unwillingness to work toward any change goals.

A *change in counselors* may have accounted for one discrepancy observed in the outcome measures, where the counselor and the investigator rated the client as unchanged but the monitoring showed some net improvement. In the one case in which this emerged, it may have been that the second counselor was unaware of the initial low status of the client; or alternatively, both counselors saw the client similarly, but the second counselor gave consistently higher ratings than the first (producing an artifactual rating of improved).

It was also noted that a very *sudden change in circumstances* could create discrepancies between the monitoring outcomes and other sources of outcome ratings. For example, if a person was institutionalized and forced to become abstinent *and* the counselor had several contacts with the client after he or she had been institutionalized, the outcome based on monitoring data would probably indicate improvement in status (i.e., positive outcome, since the institutionalized client was not drinking, was eating better, etc.); whereas the counselor might rate this a treatment failure (because the client was institutionalized). In another case, the client had no success with reducing his drinking until he voluntarily moved out of town. The case notes indicated that the client had gained insight from the treatment process and initiated the move, whereupon he became abstinent (and remained abstinent). Both the counselor and the investigator considered this case to be a treatment success. However, because of the lack of monitoring data reported after the client had moved, the outcome rating computed from monitoring data indicated that the client was unchanged.

Computing Final Outcome Ratings

The analyses of the different outcome measures suggested that the monitoring data could generate reasonably accurate outcome scores if some modifications were made to the process of computing outcome ratings. Of the 24 cases, 13 were rated as improved by all three outcome sources. For seven of the remaining 11 where differences occurred, it appeared that the monitoring data accurately portrayed events. For two additional cases, the clients improved regarding alcohol consumption but declined in other areas (consistent with the monitoring score of no change or worse). To resolve discrepancies that occurred because of the special status accorded to reducing substance use, it was decided that the alcohol use outcome score would be analyzed separately and not included in the overall change score. In addition, two changes were made in the calculations of the alcohol use change score to compensate for instances where clients were abstinent when admitted to the program (either because they came to COPA for follow-up treatment, or because they became abstinent when they first entered COPA). First, those who remained abstinent throughout treatment were classified as "improved" rather than "the same." Second, because it was sometimes not possible to discriminate whether a person's drinking became worse or whether the person had merely returned to pretreatment levels, the categories "the same" and "worse" were combined. The new ratings for progress regarding alcohol use and problems were changed to: (1) Success (both frequency of use and alcohol problem status showed improvement or the client maintained abstinence throughout treatment); (2) Partial success (either alcohol use or alcohol problems showed improvement); and (3) the Same-or-Worse (alcohol use and problem status either did not improve or appeared to become worse). Finally, those who were referred for problems other than alcohol abuse or who did not appear to have alcohol problems at admission were treated as missing on the alcohol improvement score.

To assess overall improvement, two outcome scores were used rather than one. The two outcome scores consisted of (1) a net change score in life areas other than alcohol abuse (overall classification of Improved, Same, or Deteriorated based on the sum of ratings of drug use, physical health, emotional health, mental/cognitive health, personal hygiene, accommodation status, economic status, social contacts, leisure activities, nutrition, and relationship with spouse); and (2) an alcohol improvement score (Success, Partial Success, Same-or-Worse).

Finally, for purposes of deriving a single measure of client outcomes, an overall success score was computed by combining the alcohol improvement score and the net change score in other life areas. This score consisted of four levels: (1) Improved both in alcohol use and other life areas, (2) Improved either in alcohol use or in other life areas, (3) the Same-or-Worse in alcohol use and the same in other life areas, and (4) the Same-or-Worse in alcohol use and Worse in other life areas.

These new scales were developed, and the new scores were then compared to the discharge ratings made by the COPA counselor for all 56 cases (not just the 24 analyzed from the case studies). In addition to discrepancies that were described in the previous discussion of the 24 clients who were included in the case studies, ten new discrepancies were identified. These included five cases where the counselor gave the lowest improvement rating (Moderate Improvement) and the monitoring indicated that the client was the Same (one case) or Worse (four cases). The files for these cases were examined and no evidence was found for improvement of the clients; therefore, the monitoring score was accepted as generally accurate. Of the remaining five cases, three were rated Substantially Improved by the COPA worker (two were Worse and one the Same by the monitoring method), and two were rated Successfully Maintained (both rated the Same by the monitoring method). The files for these five cases were examined with the following changes made to the monitoring scores for four of the cases: two cases were rejected from further analyses because they contained insufficient monitoring data or other information to assess what occurred with the client; for one case, the score on other life areas was changed to Improved (initially computed as the same); and for one case, the score for alcohol use was changed to Partial Success. For the remaining case, the monitoring score was accepted as accurate.

SUMMARY

The present research is an exploratory study of an innovative program, where much had to be learned about the clients and the program (by both the research staff and the program staff) as the project developed. In order to proceed with further analyses relating to client outcomes, adjustments were made to the monitoring scores to make the outcome ratings as accurate as possible. As is well known in addictions treatment evaluation, all methods of assigning outcome scores have strengths and weaknesses. In the present study, an attempt was made to compensate for some of the weaknesses in the monitoring method, by utilizing counselor discharge ratings as well as descriptive information in the files (where available). The outcome scores generated by this procedure, therefore, should provide the greatest possible accuracy in describing the progress made by clients while in the COPA program.

Chapter 9

Outcomes of Treatment at COPA

Outcomes of COPA clients will be described according to the following topics: (1) overall outcomes as computed from the monitoring data, (2) the stability of treatment outcomes (using follow-up data from the case studies), (3) the outcomes in individual life areas, and (4) the relationships of changes among the life areas.

OVERALL OUTCOMES OF COPA CLIENTS

Table 18 shows the proportions of clients who improved while in treatment, as judged by the various methods of assessing outcome. For life areas other than alcohol use, about 60 percent showed net scores of improvement and about 15 percent stayed the same. For alcohol use, about 46 percent of clients showed a successful outcome regarding both measures of alcohol use, 15 percent showed improvement on at least one alcohol measure, and 40 percent remained the same or became worse. Taking both alcohol use and other areas into consideration, about 40 percent of clients showed improvement relating both to alcohol use and to other life areas, with an additional 35 percent showing improvement in either alcohol use or other life areas (seven cases [15 percent] improved only in other life areas, and ten cases [21 percent] improved only in alcohol use). No change or deterioration was evident for about 25 percent of clients.

STABILITY OF TREATMENT OUTCOMES (COMPARISON TO FOLLOW-UP DATA FROM CASE STUDIES)

Informal follow-up data were obtained on 33 of the 36 clients included in the case studies (usually from direct interview with the

TABLE 18. Overall Outcome Scores for Clients Included in Treatment Analyses

Improvement score	Improved	Partly Improved	No change	Deteriorated
Net change score (all life areas except alcohol use) (n=54)	32 (59.3%)	- --	8 (14.8%)	14 (25.9%)
Change in alcohol use or problems (n=48)	22 (45.8%)	7 (14.6%)	19 (39.6%)[a]	- --[a]
Combination score (net change plus change in alcohol use) (n=48)	19 (39.6%)	17 (35.4%)	3 (6.3%)	9 (18.8%)

[a] For alcohol use, there was no separate category for deteriorated, as there was often insufficient information to distinguish deteriorated from no change.

client, but sometimes information was obtained from secondary sources). Although data collection for the follow-up was not sufficiently rigorous to draw firm conclusions, the data provide some limited information concerning the stability of treatment effects. The 36 cases studied were classified into three outcome categories at discharge and at follow-up: good outcome (improved), no improvement or uncertain outcome, and poor outcome (this category also included deceased from all causes as well as not being able to locate the person at follow-up). As is evident from Table 19, almost half of the cases (17 of the 36 cases) exhibited improved status at both discharge and follow-up. Also, as the table indicates, there was a definite pattern for good outcomes to be maintained at follow-up and poor or uncertain outcomes to remain poor. The follow-up was done as a supplement to the case studies and not as part of a systematic research follow-up. The time of follow-up varied from pre-discharge (i.e., the subject of the case study was still in treatment at follow-up), to several years after

TABLE 19. Relationship Between Status at Discharge and Status at Follow-up for 36 Case Studies

Status at discharge	Status at follow-up		
	Good or improved	Unimproved or uncertain status	Poor to deteriorated[a]
Good or improved	abstinent—doing well (5 cases)	would not answer questions, but known to have had at least one major relapse (1 case)	deceased (3 cases)
	occasional light drinking—doing well (3 cases)	abstinent at follow-up, but had experienced severe psychiatric problems as well as one major relapse since discharge (1 case)	
	occasional heavy drinking—doing well (3 cases)		
	apparently no problems related to drinking—consumption not reported (1 case)		
	still drinking but reduced consumption and few problems (1 case)		
	abstinent—but some health or emotional problems (3 cases)		
	abstinent from alcohol but one bout with drug addiction since discharge (1 case)		
	Total number of cases with good or improved status at both discharge and at follow-up:17	**Total number of cases with good or improved status at discharge and unimproved at follow-up: 2**	**Total number of cases with good or improved status at discharge and poor status at follow-up: 3**

TABLE 19 (continued)

Status at discharge	Status at follow-up		
	Good or improved	Unimproved or uncertain status	Poor or deteriorated[a]
Unimproved or uncertain status	abstinent–doing well (1 case) occasional heavy drinking–doing well (1 case) apparently no problems related to drinking (1 case) **Total number of cases with unimproved status at discharge and good at follow-up: 3**	would not report consumption level but believed to be drinking heavily (1 case) **Total number of cases with unimproved status at both discharge and follow-up: 2**	deceased (5 cases) institutionalized (1 case) **Total number of cases with unimproved status at discharge and poor at follow-up: 6**
Poor or deteriorated	**Total number of cases with poor status at discharge and good at follow-up: 0**	**Total number of cases with poor status at discharge and unimproved at follow-up: 0**	could not be located (3 cases) deceased (2 cases) institutionalized (1 case) too cognitively impaired to be interviewed (1 case) drinking heavily (1 case) **Total number of cases with poor status both at discharge and follow-up: 8**

[a]Including deceased and cases that could not be located.

discharge. These results, although based on informal follow-up data, provide strong evidence that changes made during treatment seemed to be maintained well (even when the client had been a long-term alcohol abuser prior to treatment).

PROPORTIONS OF CLIENTS IMPROVED
IN EACH LIFE AREA

Table 20 indicates the proportions of all clients who improved, stayed the same, or deteriorated on each of the variables employed as outcome measures. These results indicate a high proportion of clients in each life area who were unchanged. This result is not surprising, since it might be expected that many clients will remain unchanged in a particular life area because they have no problems in that life area and, therefore, do not need to change. Table 20 also shows the improvement rate for those who were initially identified as having problems in a particular life area. For some life areas, very few clients were identified as having problems at entry into treatment. For example, relationship with spouse was identified as a problem for only seven cases initially; mental/cognitive health problems for nine cases; economic problems for ten; and drug use, personal hygiene, care of clothing, care of living quarters, diet, and appetite for less than 20 cases. Of the life areas with at least 20 cases experiencing problems at intake, improvement rates varied from 57.9 percent for physical health to 40.9 percent for leisure activities (approximately half of the people who had problems seemed to improve within most life areas).

Life areas where fairly large proportions of clients deteriorated are also of interest. For example, 20 percent or more of clients deteriorated in the areas of alcohol problems, drug use, emotional health, mental/cognitive health, appetite, and relationship with spouse. For most life areas, those who deteriorated began treatment with problems rather than developing new problems while in treatment. For example, all clients who deteriorated in alcohol use, drug use, emotional health, relationship with spouse, and social/leisure activities were identified initially as having problems in these areas. Similarly, all but one of the clients who deteriorated in physical health exhibited problems initially. In a few life areas, however, new problems seemed to develop or be identified during treatment. For example, three of the six cases whose appetite deteriorated were not defined initially as having nutrition/eating problems, and all 11 of the cases whose mental/cognitive functioning deteriorated (into scores in the problem range) were not identified initially as having problems related to mental/cognitive health. Deterioration reflecting the development of new problems was also evident for a few cases in other life areas: personal hygiene (three out of six deteriorated cases were not defined as having problems initially), care of clothing (four out of six), adequacy of diet (one out of three), economic status (three out of five), and accommodation status (one out of five).

In summary, the overall trend was for improvement. Deterioration, when it occurred, was more likely to occur in clients who already had problems in that life area; the exceptions were for mental/cognitive health, where deterioration reflected new or previously unidentified problems, and for some activities of daily living, where new problems developed during treatment for some cases.

RELATIONSHIPS BETWEEN IMPROVEMENT SCORES AMONG LIFE AREAS

Table 21 shows the nonparametric correlations (using Kendall's *tau b* correlation statistic (see Methodological Issues in Examining Variables in Chapter 10)) among the improvement scores for each life area (excluding alcohol use, which is described in Table 22; and relationship with spouse, which had too few cases for analysis). These analyses were based on all cases for which improvement scores were calculated, not just those cases who had problems in that life area at admission to COPA. The numbers on which analyses were based varied from n = 20 (relationship of prescription drug use with adequacy of diet) to n = 53 (relationship of physical health with emotional health).

Significant relationships were found for the following: improvement in problems related to prescription drug use was positively related to improvements in accommodation status; improvement in physical health was positively associated with improvement in emotional health, mental/cognitive health, personal hygiene, adequacy of diet, and economic status; improvement in emotional

TABLE 20. Change in Status in Each Life Area During Treatment

Life area	Proportion improved	Proportion exhibiting no change	Proportion deteriorated	Number of cases analyzed for that life area	Proportion improved of those who had initial problems in that life area
Frequency of drinking	53.2	31.9	14.9	(n=47)	53.2 (n=47)
Alcohol problem consumption category	42.9	35.7	21.4	(n=42)	42.9 (n=42)
Drug use	12.5	66.7	20.8	(n=24)	25.0 (n=12)
Physical health	41.5	39.6	18.9	(n=53)	57.9 (n=38)
Emotional health	47.2	32.1	20.8	(n=53)	53.2 (n=47)
Mental/cognitive health	15.1	64.2	20.8	(n=53)	88.9 (n=9)
Personal hygiene	12.0	76.0	12.0	(n=50)	37.5 (n=16)
Care of clothing	14.0	74.0	12.0	(n=50)	46.7 (n=15)
Care of living quarters	23.3	63.3	13.3	(n=30)	46.7 (n=15)
Social relationships	41.4	41.4	17.2	(n=29)	46.2 (n=26)
Leisure activities	34.6	57.7	7.7	(n=26)	40.9 (n=22)
Adequacy of diet	32.1	57.1	10.7	(n=28)	69.2 (n=13)
Appetite	32.1	46.4	21.4	(n=28)	64.3 (n=14)
Economic status	21.9	62.5	15.6	(n=32)	70.0 (n=10)
Accommodation status	36.4	48.5	15.2	(n=33)	57.1 (n=21)
Relationship with spouse	25.0	41.7	33.3	(n=12)	42.9 (n=7)

TABLE 21. Relationship Between Improvement Scores for Each Life Area (Tau b Measure of Association)

Life area	Prescription drug use	Physical health	Emotional health	Mental/ cognitive	Personal hygiene
Prescription drug use	---	.40 (24)	-.30 (24)	.32 (24)	.28 (22)
Physical health		---	.28* (53)	.49*(53)	.32* (50)
Emotional health			---	.47*(53)	.19 (50)
Mental/cognitive				---	.19 (50)
Personal hygiene					
Social contacts					
Leisure activities					
Adequacy of diet					
Economic status					
Accommodation status					

Note. Number of cases on which relationship statistics were based is provided in parentheses.
*p<.05, two-tailed test of significance.

154

Life area	Social contacts	Leisure activities	Adequacy of diet	Economic status	Accommodation status
Prescription drug use	-.38 (20)	-.35 (18)	.04 (20)	.37 (21)	.46* (23)
Physical health	.04 (28)	.11 (28)	.56* (28)	.36* (31)	.28 (33)
Emotional health	.26 (28)	.21 (26)	.15 (28)	-.04 (31)	.18 (33)
Mental/cognitive	-.20 (28)	.11 (26)	.40* (28)	.34 (31)	.33 (33)
Personal hygiene	.20 (26)	.16 (24)	.34 (27)	.19 (28)	.56* (30)
Social contacts	---	.73* (25)	.12 (22)	-.44* (25)	.09 (24)
Leisure activities		---	.33 (20)	-.37 (22)	.31 (22)
Adequacy of diet			---	.40 (24)	.35 (25)
Economic status				---	.27 (30)
Accommodation status					---

Note. Number of cases on which relationship statistics were based is provided in parentheses.
*p<.05, two-tailed test of significance.

health was positively associated with improvement in mental/cognitive health; improvement in mental/cognitive health was positively associated with improvement in adequacy of diet; improvement in personal hygiene was positively associated with improvement in accommodation status; improvement in social contacts was positively associated with improvement in leisure activities and negatively with improvement in economic status.

The low numbers of cases involved in the analyses make multivariate analyses such as factor analysis unfeasible, and interpretation of these bivariate correlations needs to be done cautiously until these results have been replicated. Therefore, the following conclusions based on the results in Table 21 should be considered tentative:

- Physical health seemed to be most likely to covary with other life areas. This result seems logical in that it makes sense that a deterioration in physical health would be related to poorer functioning in other areas, especially emotional and cognitive functioning, activities of daily living (reflected by the variable personal hygiene), and diet.
- The relationship between personal hygiene and accommodation status likely reflects the relationship between the client's ability to care for himself or herself, including obtaining and keeping adequate housing.
- The high correlation between improvement in social contacts and improvement in leisure activities was expected, as the two life areas tend to be related to one another.
- Outcome in the area of mental/cognitive functioning was found to be related to emotional health and adequacy of diet. This may reflect a pattern of behavior sometimes found among older people with depression, poor cognitive functioning, and poor eating habits, since cognitive impairment is a common consequence of depression among older people.
- The *negative* relationship between improved social contacts and improved economic status was not predicted and, therefore, needs to be replicated before interpretation is justified.

Various strategies for examining the relationship between alcohol abuse and other life areas are presented in Table 22. Based on initial problem ratings (made at assessment by the COPA counselor), extent of alcohol problems was significantly and positively related to problems in the following areas at assessment: physical health, activities of daily living, and family relationships. To examine the ongoing relationship between alcohol use and problems in other life areas, correlations were calculated across ratings made at client contacts. At every contact with a client, the counselor completed a summary form rating the level of alcohol problem since last contact, as well as the client's current status, in each life area. The following life areas were found to be worse when the client's recent status regarding drinking problems appeared to be worse: physical health, emotional health, mental/cognitive health, personal hygiene, leisure activities, and adequacy of diet. Finally, significant relationships were found between the improvement score for alcohol use and improvement scores for the following life areas: mental/cognitive health, personal hygiene, adequacy of diet, and accommodation status.

Taking into consideration relationships between alcohol problems and other life areas at assessment, during treatment, and in terms of outcomes, the life areas that seemed most consistently related to status regarding extent of alcohol problems were: personal hygiene/activities of daily living, mental/cognitive health, and adequacy of diet. These relationships, plus the association between improvement in alcohol problems and improvement in accommodation status, indicate that there is likely a strong relationship between ongoing alcohol problems and the life areas most related to older persons maintaining community living, namely: mental status, care of self, diet, and accommodation.

With the exception of the single significant negative relationship, significant associations among life areas tended to be positive. These findings suggest that, although outcomes in individual life areas are of interest for certain questions, it is also legitimate and useful to consider outcomes in terms of global or overall improvement. These findings support the use and interpretation of overall outcome scores.

DISCUSSION

The present research does not provide a basis for judging the effectiveness of the COPA program in terms of other treatment programs or in terms of no treatment controls. There does not appear to be any literature that would allow for an estimate of the proportion of older persons (similar to COPA clients) who would be expected to recover from substance problems without intervention. A study by Weins et al. (1982-83) reported a high rate (about 60 percent) of older persons maintaining abstinence for one year following treatment in a hospital program. The sample consisted of first-time admissions, aged 65 and older. Since all were first admissions and most appeared to have developed problem drinking late in life, the sample was likely considerably different from the COPA sample. In a 1980 review of addictions treatment literature, Miller and Hester estimated that an average of 19 percent of problem drinkers either not seeking treatment or dropping out of treatment are abstinent or improved a year later. The follow-up data from the COPA case studies suggests that the success of COPA clients substantially exceeds this estimate of natural recovery. While these results are encouraging, a valid comparison would require natural recovery rates based on a sample similar to COPA clients. However, considering the difficulties that the present research has experienced in determining levels of alcohol use among elderly clients, believable estimates of natural recovery based on a control group would be difficult, if not impossible, to obtain.

It is equally difficult to compare these success rates to those of other addictions treatment programs. One difficulty in making comparisons is the flexible nature of the COPA program–that is, some clients receive a brief intervention while others receive long-term support and follow-up. Thus, it is difficult to know the type of program to which it should be compared. In addition, since the program has no predetermined length of treatment, there is no real concept of treatment "drop-out." Of those who might be considered dropouts, one group dropped out before ever actually engaging in the treatment process (they were excluded from the present analyses); and the second group left "against advice," but were often rated as doing quite well at discharge. Probably the most important factor that differentiates the COPA program from other addictions programs is the acceptance of people into treatment who deny their alcohol use or problems. Working with clients who do not acknowledge an addictions problem is a very unusual approach to addictions

TABLE 22. Correlations Between Status Regarding Alcohol Consumption and Status in Other Life Areas

Life area	Correlation (tau b) between alcohol problem rating at assessment and ratings of other life areas	Correlation (tau b) between level of alcohol problems prior to each contact and status in life areas at each contact[a]	Correlation (tau b) between improvement score on alcohol use and improvement scores in other life areas
Prescription drug use	.13 (n=68, p=.23)	.08 (n=351, p=.09)	-.18 (n=21, p=.42)
Physical health	.27* (n=70, p=.01)	.15* (n=550, p=.00)	.14 (n=47, p=.30)
Emotional health	.18 (n=80, p=.07)	.22* (n=553, p=.00)	.25 (n=47, p=.07)
Mental/cognitive health	---	.33* (n=550, p=.00)	.29* (n=47, p=.04)
Activities of daily living	.31* (n=69, p=.00)	---	---
Personal hygiene	.16 (n=80, p=.11)	.34* (n=531, p=.00)	.40* (n=45, p=.01)
Social contacts	.20* (n=80, p=.04)	.04 (n=401, p=.43)	.24 (n=25, p=.22)
Family relationships	.17 (n=79, p=.08)	---	---
Leisure activities	.03 (n=68, p=.77)	.11* (n=378, p=.02)	.21 (n=22, p=.33)
Nutrition	---	---	---
Adequacy of diet	-.05 (n=75, p=.59)	.33* (n=408, p=.00)	.44* (n=26, p=.02)
Economic status	.13 (n=78, p=.19)	.03 (n=400, p=.47)	.06 (n=28, p=.75)
Accommodation status	.01 (n=75, p=.94)	.02 (n=418, p=.70)	.36* (n=29, p=.04)
Relationship with spouse	.06 (n=78, p=.56)	.07 (n=167, p=.32)	---
Legal status		.06 (n=405, p=.20)	---
Overall improvement score in the areas other than alcohol use	---	---	.30* (n=48, p=.02)

[a]Analyses were performed on contacts rather than individual cases; therefore, the number on which each correlation was based refers to the number of contacts (rather than number of cases).

*p<.05, two-tailed test of significance.

treatment, and there appear to be no published comparable outcome data from programs with a similar approach. In their review of treatment literature, Miller and Hester (1980) suggested that average treatment outcomes appeared to be one-third abstinent and one-third improved at the time of discharge, with an estimate of about 26 percent successful outcomes (abstinent or improved) at 12 months after treatment. Comparison to these estimates suggest that outcomes from the COPA program are as good as average outcomes. Considering that the prevailing belief in addictions treatment is that treatment success is unlikely unless clients are willing to admit their alcohol or drug problem, the generally positive outcomes from the COPA program are even more impressive. At a minimum, these data suggest that admitting to a drinking problem may not be as critical in addictions treatment as has been generally accepted.

Chapter 10

Variables Associated with Improvement

Although many studies have attempted to identify those client variables or program variables that predict treatment success, recent reviews have concluded that there is little or no evidence for *general* predictors across programs and target populations (Edwards et al., 1988; Miller & Hester, 1986). However, as discussed by Edwards et al. (1988), there are several potential benefits of studying predictors of treatment outcome. These include: identifying who can and cannot benefit from a particular program, matching types of clients to types of programs, and identifying predictors in order to address theoretical questions. In the present context, the analyses of predictors of successful outcomes are exploratory, attempting to generate hypotheses concerning the characteristics of clients who seemed to benefit from the COPA approach. These analyses are intended to raise questions, not answer them. For example, if the data showed that more females than males improved following treatment at COPA, this finding might lead to a number of questions to guide future research such as: Are older females more responsive than older males to treatment generally? Were the COPA workers providing different, more successful treatment for females? And, do women referred to COPA exhibit a better prognosis at intake?

LITERATURE ON FACTORS ASSOCIATED WITH OUTCOMES AMONG OLDER SUBSTANCE ABUSERS

Several studies have attempted to identify predictors of outcomes among older substance abusers. Linn (1978) compared predictors of treatment dropout for younger (under age 50) and older (over age 55) clients of an inpatient (30-50 days) therapeutic community approach delivered through a Veterans Administration Hospital. She found that older clients were more likely to remain in treatment than younger clients; and that never being married and having more symptoms of introversion and depression were associated with dropping out by both younger and older clients. Several predictors of dropout showed differential relationships for older versus younger clients: older persons for whom a longer period of time had passed since their last job were more likely to drop out, while younger persons who had been unemployed longer were more likely to remain in treatment; older persons who reported feeling more inert-fatigued (at intake) were more likely to complete treatment, while younger persons who scored higher on this mood state were more likely to drop out.

Dupree, Broskowski, and Schonfeld (1984) developed a behavioral outpatient treatment program for late-onset older alcohol abusers. Although the program was highly successful with program completers, they experienced a high rate of program dropouts (50 percent). Their analyses indicated that dropouts were more likely to exhibit the following characteristics at intake: a lower estimate of probable success in the program, more "external" locus of control, higher depression scores, and self-report of drinking larger quantities of alcohol.

Helzer, Carey, and Miller (1984) compared predictors of long-term outcomes (six to ten-10 year follow-up after treatment) from four addictions treatment programs (inpatient and outpatient) for younger (age 59 and younger) versus older (age 60 and over) clients. They found that the following were significant predictors of better outcomes for older clients, but not for younger clients: being married or cohabiting, not living alone, being assessed as dual diagnosis (i.e., alcoholism plus some other psychiatric disorder), a history of depression, evidence of cognitive impairment, and grandparents born within the U.S. Being unemployed for six months or more was significantly associated with poor outcomes for both age groups. The results from these studies are summarized in Table 23. As is evident from this table, the small existing literature on predictors of successful treatment of older substance abusers has tended to focus on client characteristics as predictors, with no overall pattern emerging.

TABLE 23. Summary of Literature on Predictors of Successful Outcomes of Addictions Treatment for Older Persons

Type of Outcome Measure	Predictor
Program completion	–having been married at some time –less symptoms of introversion –less symptoms of depression/lower depression scores –shorter duration since last job –more likely to report feeling tired at intake –perception by client of higher likelihood of success in the program –lower "external" locus of control –self-report of drinking less alcohol
Good long-term outcome	–being married or cohabiting[a] –not living alone[a] –being assessed as dual diagnosis[a] –history of depression[a] –evidence of cognitive impairment[a] –grandparents born within U.S.[a] –not being unemployed for 6 months or more[a]

[a]These measures were all taken at the time of the follow-up interview (5-8 years after treatment)

This chapter will examine the relationship between overall outcomes and demographic variables (age, sex, marital status), program variables (referral source, referral type, number of contacts, number of days in COPA program), and client characteristics at the time of initial assessment (e.g., severity of problems).

METHODOLOGICAL ISSUES IN EXAMINING VARIABLES RELATED TO OUTCOMES

The following sections describe the results of correlational analyses of variables that may have contributed to the client's outcome of treatment at COPA. Most analyses include two types of outcome measures: (1) improved status related to alcohol use, and (2) overall improvement in life areas other than alcohol use. The correlation statistic used in most of these analyses is Kendall's *tau b*. Because most variables consist of rating scales that provide ordinal, but not necessarily interval, data, a nonparametric measure of association (such as *tau b*) was chosen as most appropriate. *Tau b* varies from -1.00 to $+1.00$ depending on the extent to which two variables are related to one another, with numbers closer to $+1.00$ indicating that two variables are positively associated, 0.00 indicating no association, and numbers towards -1.00 indicating that the two variables are negatively associated. Because of the small sample size and the exploratory nature of the analyses, all results are presented as bivariate relationships, and no adjustment of significance level ($p < .05$, two-tailed) was made for the large number of relationships analyzed. These estimates of bivariate relationships provide the clearest basis for replication in future studies. Although no multivariate statistics will be used to summarize findings, interpretation of bivariate results will involve examining relationships for interpretable patterns rather than extensive interpretation of individual significant relationships.

Use of Improvement Scores

This study was different from most outcome studies of addictions treatment in that it used improvement scores rather than absolute outcomes (e.g., abstinence). Linn (1978) and Dupree, Broskowski, and Schonfeld (1984) used completing treatment (an absolute rather than relative measure) as their measure of outcome. Helzer, Carey, and Miller (1984) also defined successful outcomes using a posttest measure only. Thus, none of the previous studies reviewed measured outcome as a function of initial status. For the COPA study, however, improvement scores seemed the most appropriate. Treatment goals were set according to the client's individual circumstances rather than according to standard goals that all clients were intended to achieve.

The use of improvement scores, while justified for the present study, changes the interpretation of results somewhat when correlates are examined. In particular, there is an inherent bias that those who are initially the most poorly-off will be those most likely to improve during treatment, either because initial functioning was unusually poor and improvement would have occurred anyway, or because the higher the initial functioning the less room there would be for improvement. On the other hand, using absolute measures of outcome tends to bias results in the opposite direction. For example, if the measure of success regarding physical health is a rating of good to very good health, it is obvious that those who are initially in the best health are the most likely to be able to achieve this criterion.

The existing literature on predictors of treatment outcome among older people used two different types of outcome measures: treatment completion, and long-term outcomes without comparison to initial status. This literature indicated no interpretable pattern of outcomes. The COPA study used a third type of outcome measure: improvement relative to initial status. That is, a successful outcome for these analyses did not necessarily mean that the client reached an optimal level of functioning.

RELATIONSHIP OF CLIENT DEMOGRAPHIC VARIABLES WITH IMPROVEMENT

Table 24 shows the relationships between gender, age, and marital status and (1) the alcohol improvement score, and (2) the overall improvement score for life areas other than alcohol use. As is apparent from this table, the only significant relationship that emerged between demographic variables and these two outcome measures was for age, where there was a significant trend for younger persons to score more positively on the overall improvement score for life areas other than alcohol use.

These results indicate that there is no strong effect of marital status on outcome, although the small literature on predictors of outcomes for older people would suggest a positive advantage to being married. It may be that the sample of persons of each marital status in the present study was too small to identify a pattern regarding outcome.

The negative relationship between age and outcome in life areas other than alcohol use may be attributable to the negative relationship between age and physical health. Analyses of the relationship between age and outcome in each life area indicated a significant

TABLE 24. Correlations (tau b) of Demographic Variables with Outcomes

Variable	Alcohol score		Overall improvement for life areas other than alcohol	
	tau b	n	tau b	n
Gender (1. males, 2. females)	-.23	48	.07	54
Age in years	-.14	48	-.23	54
	Cramers's V[a]	n	Cramer's V[a]	n
Marital status (single, married, separated/divorced, widowed)	.27	48	.33	54

*p<.05
[a]significance level assessed using Chi-squared statistic

negative relationship between age and improved physical health (*tau b* = − .43, n = 53, p < .05); that is, younger clients were more likely than older clients to improve in the area of physical health. Age was not significantly related to outcomes in any other life areas.

RELATIONSHIP OF PROGRAM VARIABLES WITH IMPROVEMENT

As is shown in Table 25, improvement regarding use of alcohol was associated with more contacts with the COPA counselor and being in the program longer. Extent of treatment was not significantly related to overall outcome in life areas other than alcohol use, and referral source was not significantly associated with either of the major outcome variables. The size of relationship between alcohol use and extent of treatment was modest and open to several possible interpretations. It may be that greater improvement is associated with more treatment. It may also be that those who receive more treatment started out with more severe alcohol prob-

TABLE 25. Correlations (tau b) of Program Variables with Outcomes

Variable	Alcohol improvement score		Improvement score for life areas other than alcohol	
	tau b	*n*	*tau b*	*n*
Number of contacts with COPA counselor	.33*	48	.18	54
Number of days in COPA program (from initial visit to discharge)	.24*	48	.16	54
Referral Source (visiting nurse, other medical, family or friend, self, other)	*Cramer's V*[a] .14	*n* 48	*Cramer's V*[a] .21	*n* 54

*p<.05
[a]significance level assessed using Chi-squared statistic

lems and were therefore more likely to show improvement. Finally, it is possible that those who reduced alcohol use stayed in treatment longer because they generally were more cooperative clients.

RELATIONSHIP BETWEEN IMPROVEMENT SCORES AND ALCOHOL USE VARIABLES MEASURED AT ASSESSMENT

Of the 32 variables regarding alcohol use recorded at assessment and four addictions treatment variables, five alcohol-use variables were found to predict improvement in alcohol use, and six different alcohol-use variables were associated with improved status in life areas other than alcohol use (see Table 26). Improved status regarding alcohol use was associated with clients who reported starting drinking regularly at a younger age, clients whose moods did not appear to be affected by alcohol use, clients who were willing to answer questions concerning their recent consumption of alcohol, clients who were willing to answer questions concerning the effects on them of alcohol consumption, and clients who were rated as having more severe alcohol problems. These results and the general pattern of correlations indicate that those who were most open about their drinking and drinking problems, and those whose problems appeared more severe at assessment, were more likely to show improvement regarding alcohol use. It is likely that at least part of this relationship is artifactual; that is, those who had more severe problems initially had the most room to improve. Nevertheless, the results do not support the assumption that those with less severe problems are more responsive to treatment. In fact, these results are consistent with informal observations made by COPA counselors that even some of the seemingly most intransigent cases (e.g., long-term skid row cases) could show measurable improvement with treatment.

Improvement in life areas other than alcohol use was associated with the following patterns of alcohol use at the time of assessment: higher usual consumption, higher maximum consumption, being more likely to use alcohol to relieve tension or anxiety, a lack of denial of excessive use and negative consequences of alcohol, and the client expressing more concern than other clients about his or her own alcohol problems. Although variables emerged which were different from those associated with improvement in alcohol use, a similar pattern of relationships was apparent: the greater the alcohol problem and the lower the denial, the more likely that the client improved in other life areas. Again, these results provide no support for the argument that those who have more severe alcohol problems will have a poorer prognosis.

RELATIONSHIP BETWEEN IMPROVEMENT SCORES AND DRUG USE VARIABLES MEASURED AT ASSESSMENT

Of the drug use variables that were measured, use of sleeping pills and benzodiazepines was associated with improved scores on alcohol use, while the use of anticonvulsants was associated with poorer outcomes in life areas other than alcohol use (see Table 27).

TABLE 26. Correlations (tau b) of Alcohol Use Variables (Measured at Assessment) with Outcomes

Variable	Alcohol Improvement score		Overall Improvement score for life area other than alcohol	
	tau b	n	tau b	n
Whether there were times client drank more (1. yes, 0. no)	.28	35	.27	37
Whether client had ever abstained for a significant length of time (1. yes, 0. no)	.33	32	.14	32
Frequency of drinking (reported by client) (1. less than once a month to 9. three or more times a day)	.23	37	.14	39
Frequency of drinking (reported by other source) (1. less than once a month to 9. three or more times a day)	.16	26	-.14	27
Client's report of consumption during past week (total number of standard drinks)[a]	.17	29	.16	31
Client's report of usual consumption (in standard drinks)[a]	.23	31	.39*	33
Client's report of maximum consumption (in standard drinks)[a]	.11	27	.50*	30
Client reports that alcohol relieves tension/anxiety (1. yes, 0. no)	-.08	38	.35*	40
Client reports that alcohol relieves pain (1. yes, 0. no)	.03	38	-.18	40
Client reports that alcohol makes him/her more sociable (1. yes, 0. no)	.01	38	.26	40
Client reports that alcohol relaxes him/her (1. yes, 0. no)	.20	38	.25	40
Client reports that alcohol blocks out depressing thoughts (1. yes, 0. no)	.18	38	.22	40
Client reports that he/she just drinks to be sociable (1. yes, 0. no)	-.11	38	-.09	40
Age when client started drinking regularly (in years)	-.31*	28	-.04	29
Whether client's drinking affecting health (1. yes, 0. no)	.06	41	-.10	43
Whether client's drinking affecting ability to get around (1. yes, 0. no)	-.01	41	.17	43
Whether client's drinking affecting moods (1. yes, 0. no)	-.33*	41	-.23	43
Whether client's drinking affecting memory (1. yes, 0. no)	.02	41	.06	43
Whether client's drinking affecting getting along with others (1. yes, 0. no)	.04	41	-.16	43
Whether cutting down on drinking would improve health, mood, etc. (1. yes, 0. no)	.16	41	.03	43
Whether client currently experiences dependence symptoms from drinking (1. yes, 0. no)	-.12	39	-.24	41
Whether client currently experiences health problems from drinking (1. yes, 0. no)	-.25	39	-.23	41
Whether client currently experiences problem-drinking patterns (1. yes, 0. no)	-.06	39	-.21	41
Whether client currently experiences problems due to behavior when intoxicated (1. yes, 0. no)	.22	39	-.09	41

TABLE 26 (continued)

Variable	Alcohol Improvement score		Overall Improvement score for life area other than alcohol	
	tau b	n	tau b	n
Whether client currently experiences other problems related to alcohol consumption (1. yes, 0. no)	-.12	39	-.28	41
Whether client is willing to reduce alcohol consumption (1. yes, 0. no)	.21	35	.08	37
Whether client denies apparent negative consequences of alcohol consumption (1. not at all, 2. somewhat, 3. a great deal)	-.17	42	-.39*	40
Whether client denies excessive use of alcohol (1. not at all, 2. somewhat, 3. a great deal)	-.23	42	-.33*	44
Whether client reported recent consumption (1. yes, 0. no)	.37*	48	.04	54
Whether client reported effects of alcohol consumption (1. yes, 0. no.)	.30*	48	-.06	54
Client's concern about problems regarding drinking alcohol (1. not at all to 5. extremely)	.06	39	.27*	41
Interviewer's rating of client's need for assistance regarding alcohol problems (1. client strength to 6. extreme crisis)	.29*	43	-.08	46
Addictions treatment history				
Whether client has received assistance for alcohol problems during the past 6 months (1. yes, 0. no)	-.21	41	-.01	43
Whether client has ever received assistance for alcohol problems (1. yes, 0. no)	.11	41	.10	43
Whether client has ever been admitted to a detox (for alcohol or drugs) (1. yes, 0. no)	.19	43	.03	48
Whether client has ever received some form of addictions treatment (for alcohol or drugs) (1. yes, 0. no)	-.09	43	.02	48

[a] A standard drink was defined as 12 oz. beer (5% alcohol), 1 1/2 oz. liquor (40% alcohol), 5 oz. table wine (about 12% alcohol), or 3 oz. sherry (18-20% alcohol).
*p<.05.

The finding that those who were taking minor tranquilizers and sleeping pills were more likely to improve in regard to their alcohol abuse may again reflect the role of initial severity of problem–that is, it is possible that those who were taking psychoactive drugs had more severe alcohol problems or were more open about their initial levels of alcohol and drug use. These findings would, therefore, be consistent with the trend for improvement regarding alcohol abuse to be associated with greater initial severity of alcohol problems.

RELATIONSHIP BETWEEN IMPROVEMENT SCORES AND PHYSICAL HEALTH AND NUTRITION VARIABLES MEASURED AT ASSESSMENT

Only one physical health variable (having at least one physical health problem related to alcohol consumption) was significantly associated with improvement scores (see Table 28). Again, the manner in which the presence of physical health problems related to alcohol consumption may reflect a greater severity of alcohol problems at entry to COPA or a greater openness about problems. No significant relationships were found between improvement scores and initial nutritional status or use of tobacco or caffeine.

RELATIONSHIP BETWEEN IMPROVEMENT SCORES AND EMOTIONAL/MENTAL HEALTH VARIABLES MEASURED AT ASSESSMENT

As shown in Table 29, although a large number of variables were examined, only a few predicted outcomes. Clients who reported feeling tense or anxious, difficulty sleeping, and trouble concentrating at the time of entry into COPA were more likely to show improvement in alcohol use; and clients who were more concerned about their emotional health problems were more likely to exhibit improvement in life areas other than alcohol use. These results do not seem to form an interpretable pattern. In addition, there was no evidence to support previous findings that depression or cognitive impairment influenced outcomes.

TABLE 27. Correlations (tau b) of Drug Use Variables (Measured at Assessment or During Treatment) with Outcomes

Variable	Alcohol Improvement score		Overall Improvement score for life areas other than alcohol	
	tau b	n	tau b	n
Use of the following:				
Sleeping pills/barbiturates (1. yes, 0. no)	.29*	48	.01	54
Benzodiazepines/antianxiety (1. yes, 0. no)	.30*	48	-.01	54
Antidepressant (1. yes, 0. no)	-.09	48	-.10	54
Analgesics (1. yes, 0. no)	.18	48	-.18	54
Anticonvulsants (1. yes, 0. no)	-.15	48	-.26*	54
Antipsychotics/major tranquilizers (1. yes, 0. no)	.08	48	-.07	54
Respiratory-allergy (1. yes, 0. no)	.12	48	-.16	54
Hypertension medications (1. yes, 0. no)	-.08	48	.03	54
Heart medicine (1. yes, 0. no)	.23	48	.06	54
Other prescription drugs (1. yes, 0. no)	.19	48	-.10	54
Client's concern about problems regarding prescription drug use (1. not at all to 5. extremely)	.03	31	.12	36
Interviewer's rating of client's need for assistance regarding use of prescription drugs (1. client strength to 6. extreme crisis)	.16	42	.01	47

*p<.05

TABLE 28. Correlations (tau b) of Physical Health and Nutrition Variables Including Use of Tobacco and Caffeine (Measured at Assessment) with Outcomes

Variable	Alcohol Improvement score		Overall Improvement score for life areas other than alcohol	
	tau b	n	tau b	n
At least one physical health problem related to client's alcohol consumption (1. yes, 0. no)	.35*	42	.26	47
Client's concern about problems regarding physical health (1. not at all to 5. extremely)	.02	42	.07	47
Interviewer's rating of client's need for assistance regarding physical health (1. client strength to 6. extreme crisis)	.06	43	.05	48
Client's rating of his/her diet (1. very poor to 7. excellent)	-.18	43	-.19	48
Interviewer's rating of the adequacy of client's diet (1. very poor to 7. excellent)	-.02	42	-.09	47
Client's rating of his/her appetite (1. very poor to 7. excellent)	-.12	43	-.20	48
Client's concern about problems regarding nutrition (1. not at all to 5. extremely)	.20	42	.19	47
Interviewer's rating of client's need for assistance regarding nutrition (1. client strength to 6. extreme crisis)	.07	43	.06	48
Use of tobacco (1. yes, 0. no)	-.03	43	.12	48
Use of coffee (1. yes, 0. no)	.20	43	.22	48
Use of tea (1. yes, 0. no)	.16	43	.04	48

*$p<.05$.

TABLE 29. Correlations (tau b) of Emotional/Mental Health (Measured at Assessment) with Outcomes

Variable	Alcohol Improvement score		Overall Improvement score for life areas other than alcohol	
	tau b	n	tau b	n
Tension/anxiety (1. yes, 0. no)	.39*	46	.00	52
Difficulty eating (1. yes, 0. no)	.14	44	.07	50
Difficulty sleeping (1. yes, 0. no)	.30*	44	.07	50
Depression (1. yes, 0. no)	.05	47	.01	53
Loneliness (1. yes, 0. no)	.08	47	.08	53
Irrational fears/phobias (1. yes, 0. no)	.21	35	.07	41
Trouble concentrating (1. yes, 0. no)	.35*	38	.13	44
Feeling people are against you (1. yes, 0. no)	.04	35	-.29	41
Feeling inferior to others (1. yes, 0. no)	.16	32	.12	38
Having uncontrollable thoughts/impulses (1. yes, 0. no)	-.05	26	-.11	31
Feeling aggressive (1. yes, 0. no)	.12	32	-.19	37
Having thoughts of suicide (1. yes, 0. no)	.26	30	-.05	36
Having sexual problems (1. yes, 0. no)	.04	27	-.01	32
Feeling preoccupied/forgetful (1. yes, 0. no)	.14	37	.15	42
Amnesia/trouble remembering past events (1. yes, 0. no)	.19	34	-.03	39
Client's concern about problems regarding emotional health (1. not at all to 5. extremely)	.23	39	.43*	44
Interviewer's rating of client's need for assistance regarding emotional health (1. client strength to 6. extreme crisis)	.06	43	.02	48

*p<.05

Table 30 shows the relationship between improvement scores and ratings made by the counselor of the client's emotional/mental well-being during the assessment interviews. Only one rating was found to be significantly related to outcome: more cooperative clients tended to show more improvement for life areas other than alcohol use.

RELATIONSHIP BETWEEN IMPROVEMENT SCORES AND INITIAL STATUS REGARDING ACTIVITIES OF DAILY LIVING

None of the measures of activities of daily living recorded at the time of assessment was significantly associated with improvement in alcohol use or overall improvement in other life areas (see Table 31).

RELATIONSHIP BETWEEN IMPROVEMENT SCORES AND SOCIAL/LEISURE, FAMILY, AND MARITAL VARIABLES MEASURED AT ASSESSMENT

Only one of the six social/leisure variables showed a significant relationship with improved status: the less that a client was socially isolated (i.e., the more likely the client was to report having close friends) at the time of assessment, the more likely the client was to show overall improvement in life areas other than alcohol use. This was one of the largest relationships identified in the outcome analyses. This would appear to indicate that the client's pretreatment level of social support affects the client's ability to improve in treatment. This suggests that even the COPA outreach approach has limited success with clients who are very socially isolated. None of the family or marital variables showed a significant relationship with improvement scores (see Table 32).

TABLE 30. Correlations (tau b) of Counselor's Ratings at Assessment with Outcomes

Rating Scale	Alcohol Improvement score		Overall improvement score for life areas other than alcohol	
	tau b	n	tau b	n
Appearance (1. very unkempt to 7. very well-groomed)	.18	43	.14	48
Attitude (1. very uncooperative to 7. very cooperative)	.07	43	.27*	48
Orientation (1. very disoriented to 7. well oriented)	.11	43	-.05	48
Memory (1. great difficulty remembering to 7. excellent memory)	.19	43	.03	48
Speech (1. great difficulty speaking to 7. fluent and articulate)	.10	43	.02	48
Mood (1. very sad to 7. very happy)	.00	43	-.09	48
Energy level (1. very lethargic to 7. very energetic)	.01	43	.14	48
Concentration (1. very distracted to 7. good concentration)	.11	43	.06	48
Intoxication (1. appeared very intoxicated to 7. appeared completely sober)	.08	43	.13	48

*p<.05.

TABLE 31. Correlations (tau b) of Variables Related to Activities of Daily Living (Measured at Assessment) with Outcomes

Variable	Alcohol Improvement score		Overall Improvement score for life areas other than alcohol	
	tau b	n	tau b	n
Personal hygiene (1. poor to 5. excellent)	-.01	42	.13	47
Care of clothing (1. poor to 5. excellent)	-.01	42	.15	47
Care of living quarters (1. poor to 5. excellent)	-.12	36	.24	41
Food preparation (1. poor to 5. excellent)	-.20	37	.14	41
Use of telephone (1. poor to 5. excellent)	-.02	38	.09	42
Ability to conduct shopping (1. poor to 5. excellent)	-.04	37	.01	41
Ability to do banking (1. poor to 5. excellent)	-.14	31	.01	34
Ability to use methods of transportation (1. poor to 5. excellent)	.01	40	-.01	43
Client's concern about problems regarding activities of daily living (1. not at all to 5. extremely)	-.01	43	.16	48
Interviewer's rating of client's need for assistance regarding activities of daily living (1. client strength to 6. extreme crisis)	-.08	43	-.04	48

*p<.05.

177

TABLE 32. Correlations (tau b) of Social/Leisure, Family, and Marital Variables (Measured at Assessment) with Outcome

Variable	Alcohol Improvement score		Overall improvement score for life areas other than alcohol	
	tau b	n	tau b	n
Extent that client is socially isolated (higher number means <u>less</u> socially isolated) (1. no social contacts to 4. close friends)	.07	28	.56*	32
Whether client has problems with friends or problems acquiring friends (1. yes, 0. no)	.04	36	.13	39
Client's concern about problems regarding social relationships (1. not at all to 5. extremely)	.09	39	.19	43
Interviewer's rating of client's need for assistance regarding social relationships (1. client strength to 6. extreme crisis)	.00	43	.13	48
Client's concern about problems regarding leisure activities (1. not at all to 5. extremely)	.18	40	.15	44
Interviewer's rating of client's need for assistance regarding leisure activities (1. client strength to 6. extreme crisis)	.02	42	.07	47
Whether client has family members who have ever had alcohol or drug problems (1. yes, 0. no)	.01	29	.00	34
Client's concern about problems regarding family relationships (1. not at all to 5. extremely)	-.13	38	-.01	43
Interviewer's rating of client's need for assistance regarding family relationships (1. client strength to 6. extreme crisis)	-.02	43	-.04	48
Whether client has marital problems (1. yes, 0. no)	.26	38	.11	42
Satisfaction with relationship with spouse (1. very satisfactory to 5. very unsatisfactory)	-.35	22	-.13	22
Client's concern about problems regarding relationship with spouse (1. not at all to 5. extremely)	.02	33	-.02	37
Interviewer's rating of client's need for assistance regarding relationship with spouse (1. client strength to 6. extreme crisis)	.11	41	-.02	46

*$p < .05$.

RELATIONSHIP BETWEEN IMPROVEMENT SCORES AND ECONOMIC, ACCOMMODATION, EMPLOYMENT/EDUCATION, AND LEGAL VARIABLES MEASURED AT ASSESSMENT

Economic and Accommodation Variables

None of the measures of economic status predicted outcome. However, significant relationships were found between improvement scores and three of the seven accommodation variables: type of housing, nonpermanent accommodation, and living alone (see Table 33). Type of housing was classified to reflect a gradient of social stability: (1) own home, (2) rented house or apartment, and (3) other (boarding house, nursing home). The significant relationship between type of housing and alcohol abuse indicates that the less socially-stable clients tended to improve more regarding alcohol abuse. Consistent with this, the analyses indicated a significant relationship between improved alcohol use and reporting of nonpermanent accommodation at the time of admission to COPA. As with the prediction of outcome by some alcohol-use variables, the relationship between social stability and improved status regarding alcohol use may be an artifact of openness at the time of assessment regarding severity of drinking problems. It seems likely that the less socially-stable older person may be more open than the socially-stable person regarding alcohol use and associated problems. Therefore, less socially-stable clients may be rated as having more severe alcohol problems at assessment and, therefore, would be more likely to demonstrate improvement. These results, however, suggest that lack of social stability is *not* an impediment to treatment among older people. There is reason to believe that programs like COPA may be particularly timely for persons of low social stability. In Ontario (and likely elsewhere), old age security provides a higher and more easily obtained income than general welfare. At least some skid row clients at COPA were able to achieve some respectability through increased income at pensionable age, through some help from the COPA counselor in finding appropriate housing, and so on. This transition to more conventional living among skid row clients often seemed to include a decrease in problematic drinking. The analyses also showed a significant relation-

TABLE 33. Correlations (tau b) of Economic, Accommodation, Employment/Education, and Legal Variables (Measured at Assessment) with Outcomes

Variable	Alcohol Improvement score		Overall Improvement score for life areas other than alcohol	
	tau b	n	tau b	n
Financial status				
Whether client has had financial problems during past 6 months (1. yes, 0. no)	.09	42	.32	47
Client's concern about problems regarding finances (1. not at all to 5. extremely)	.01	42	.16	47
Interviewer's rating of client's need for assistance regarding finances (1. client strength to 6. extreme crisis)	.02	42	.23	47
Accommodation				
Type of housing (1. own home, 2. rented house/apt., 3. other)	.39*	43	.00	48
Whether client is living alone (1. yes, 0. no)	.01	42	.35*	47
Whether accommodation is permanent (1. yes, 0. no)	-.35*	43	.03	48
Satisfaction with living arrangements (1. very satisfactory to 5. very unsatisfactory)	.18	43	-.15	47
Whether any cohabitants had drinking/drug problems (1. yes, 0. no)	-.08	30	-.14	31
Client's concern about problems regarding accommodation (1. not at all to 5. extreme)	.21	40	.00	44
Interviewer's rating of client's needs for assistance regarding accommodation (1. client strength to 6. extreme crisis)	.10	43	-.07	48
Employment/education				
Extent that client is satisfied with present employment status (1. very satisfied to 5. very unsatisfied)	.33*	34	.25	39
Highest education level completed (1. special education to 8. university completed)	-.04	27	-.09	31
General effect of no longer working (1. very pleasant to 5. very upsetting)	.14	32	.19	36
Client's concern about problems regarding employment status (1. not at all to 5. extreme)	-.01	35	.17	37
Interviewer's rating of client's need for assistance regarding employment status (1. client strength to 6. extreme crisis)	-.02	42	.11	47

Variable	Alcohol Improvement score		Overall improvement score for life areas other than alcohol	
	tau b	*n*	*tau b*	*n*
Legal status				
Whether client has any current legal problems (1. yes, 0. no)	-.08	41	-.04	46
Client's concern about problems regarding legal status (1. not at all to 5. extreme)	-.07	32	.10	33
Interviewer's rating of client's need for assistance regarding legal status (1. client strength to 6. extreme crisis)	.03	43	-.12	48

*p<.05.

ship between living alone at the time of admission to COPA and overall improvement in life areas other than alcohol use, which is the opposite of what was found in the study by Helzer, Carey, and Miller (1984) of long-term outcomes.

Employment/Education and Legal Variables

Of the six employment/education variables, a significant relationship was found between level of satisfaction with present employment status and alcohol improvement: the more dissatisfied the client was with his or her employment status, the more likely he or she improved regarding alcohol abuse (see Table 33). No significant relationships were found between outcomes and legal variables.

DISCUSSION

Table 34 shows a summary of the client variables measured at assessment that were found to predict improvement. In addition to these variables, two other variables were found to predict improvement regarding alcohol use: number of contacts with the COPA counselor and duration of time in the COPA program. The following discussion summarizes the main trends indicated by these data.

> • *The small number of significant relationships suggest that there is little basis for predicting outcomes among older substance abusers.*

What was perhaps most noteworthy about these analyses was the very small number of variables that were found to predict outcomes. Given the large number of variables analyzed, there were surprisingly few significant findings. Furthermore, of the significant relationships observed, an even smaller group of significant findings could be interpreted as patterns or trends, rather than random variations. Since the sample for the present study was small, it is important that these results be replicated. Nevertheless, it may well be that among older substance abusers, there is little basis for predicting who will respond to treatment. Certainly the case studies,

TABLE 34. A Summary of Significant Relationships Between Improvement and Client Variables Measured at Assessment

Type of predictor	Alcohol improvement score	Improvement score for life areas other than alcohol
	Those who improved were more likely to:	
demographic	• be younger	
alcohol use	• have begun drinking regularly at younger age • report that alcohol was not affecting mood • be willing to report alcohol consumption and alcohol effects • be rated by worker as having a more severe alcohol problem	• report higher usual alcohol consumption • report higher maximum consumption • use alcohol to relieve tension or anxiety • admit to excessive use or negative consequences of alcohol • express higher concern alcohol problems
drug use	• use benzodiazepines and sleeping pills	• not use anticonvulsants
physical health	• have at least one physical health problem related to alcohol consumption	
emotional health	• report feeling tense or anxious • report difficulty sleeping • report trouble concentrating	• express higher concern about emotional problems • be rated by worker as more cooperative
social/leisure		• be less socially isolated
accommodation	• live in other accommodation than house or apartment • be in non-permanent accommodation	• be living alone
employment	• be dissatisfied with employment status	

as well as informal discussions with the clinical staff, have indicated that subjectively it is difficult to predict at assessment who will succeed. Some of the cases who initially appeared to be the most hopeless made surprising gains, while other cases with apparently modest problems sometimes showed rapid deterioration regardless of the counselor's efforts.

• *Clients who are more open and concerned about their problems and more cooperative tend to show better outcomes from treatment.*

Although some clients who improved denied or avoided discussion of substance problems, there was a general trend for good outcomes to be associated with: openness about alcohol consumption and its consequences, being cooperative initially and during treatment, and showing greater concern about resolving their problems. Although the COPA approach has demonstrated that admission of substance problems is not a necessary prerequisite of successful treatment, these findings indicate that acknowledgement of the problem and willingness to work on problems are definitely helpful in achieving improvement.

• *Those having more serious problems with alcohol or drugs are as likely (or possibly more likely) to respond to treatment.*

A number of variables indicated that those whose initial substance problem was more severe were more likely to exhibit improved status at follow-up. These variables included: starting regular drinking at an earlier age, higher reported consumption levels, higher rating by the worker of severity of alcohol problems, more likely to be using benzodiazepines and sleeping pills, and more likely to have at least one physical health problem related to alcohol consumption. However, there are several difficulties in interpreting relationships between improved status and initial severity. One problem relates to the general use of improvement scores. Since persons who begin treatment with worse problems have more room for improvement than those whose problems are minor, improvement scores have an inherent bias in demonstrating effects for more problematic clients. Another problem is that the relationship between initial severity and improvement may actually reflect the relationship between initial openness about problems and improvement. That is, some of the clients who improved may not really have had more severe substance problems initially, but may have only *seemed* to have more severe problems because of their willingness to admit high alcohol consumption and problem consequences. However, secondary analyses of the data did not support the argument that the relationship between improvement scores and alcohol problem severity measures was related to greater openness about alcohol use. Only one severity measure was consistently related to measures of openness; namely, the client's report of higher maximum number of drinks on any one occasion was significantly associated with the following variables that measured some aspect of openness: lack of denial of excessive alcohol use and of negative consequences, higher concern about alcohol problems, and higher average ratings during treatment on cooperativeness and openness. None of the other measures of alcohol problem severity exhibited significant relationships with variables reflecting openness about alcohol problems. Nevertheless, given the potential alternative explanations of cause and effect, a conservative interpretation of the results is that those who have more severe substance problems are *at least* as likely to respond to treatment as those with less severe problems.

- *Among elderly substance abusers, less socially-stable clients respond to treatment as well or better than more socially-stable clients.*

COPA counselors had reported informally that they felt they were as successful or even more successful with skid row or less socially-stable clients as with the more socially-stable clients. The results from the research tended to support this observation. Successful outcomes (particularly with regard to alcohol use) tended to be associated with poorer and nonpermanent accommodations. These results are inconsistent with other findings in the literature, where, if anything, better outcomes tend to be associated with higher social stability (Ogborne, 1978). Again, these results may be partly attributable to the use of improvement scores (i.e., less socially-stable clients may be worse off with regard to alcohol use at the time of admission to the program, and therefore be more likely to "improve"). Alternatively, clients who were more socially-stable may have been less willing to report heavy alcohol use at the time of entry into treatment, and, therefore, the alcohol improvement score would be underestimated for more socially-stable clients. Secondary analyses did not support either of these interpretations. There was only one significant correlation between accommodation measures and alcohol problem severity measures taken at assessment; this consisted of a significant positive relationship between usual number of drinks reported at assessment and average severity rating of accommodation problems during treatment. Otherwise, no relationship between alcohol problems and accommodation problems emerged. Similarly, the correlations of four accommodation variables with seven openness variables identified only one significant relationship: a significant positive association between poor level of housing at assessment and average rating of cooperativeness during treatment. The lack of overall relationship between accommodation status (or social stability) and other predictor variables suggests that lower social stability may be a positive contributor to readiness to change among older substance abusers.

- *Clients who remain in treatment longer are more likely to show improvement, and tend to be more open and cooperative during treatment.*

As previously shown in Table 25, those who received more treatment were significantly more likely to show improvement regarding alcohol use. This cannot necessarily be interpreted to mean that more treatment is beneficial. As with other relationships identified, cause and effect are impossible to determine. It may be that those who do not improve in these life areas drop out of treatment earlier or are discharged earlier. Finney, Moos, and Chan (1981) suggested that to identify treatment effects in correlational analyses, partial correlations should be used to control for predictive antecedent variables. In the present study, however, background variables concerning pretreatment functioning did not tend to be highly predictive of outcomes. Therefore, rather than using partial correlations, secondary bivariate correlations were conducted to identify convergence of predictor variables. One cluster of variables that was predictive of improved status and *also* tended to be related to duration of treatment were the variables that measured the client's openness to acknowledging a substance problem and cooperativeness with the worker. In short, it was found that both openness regarding substance use and longer duration in treatment predicted better outcomes.

Further analyses also indicated that there was a significant relationship between openness and length of time in treatment. Although not all variables measuring openness or cooperativeness were significantly related to treatment duration variables, enough relationships were observed to suggest a pattern. Using two-tailed tests of significance and Kendall's *tau b* as a measure of association, the following were found to be significantly related: *number of days in treatment* was related to the client being willing to report the past week's alcohol consumption at assessment, and to higher average ratings on cooperativeness and openness during treatment; *number of contacts with the COPA worker* was associated with willingness to report alcohol consumption and alcohol effects (at assessment), and to higher average ratings of cooperativeness and openness during treatment. There was also some evidence that treatment duration was related to initial alcohol problem severity, with number of contacts related to: a higher rating of alcohol problem severity by the worker at assessment, and to the greater likelihood of having at least one physical health problem related to alcohol consumption. It seems reasonable to conclude that clients stay in treatment longer *because* they are more cooperative or less resistant, and possibly *because* they have a more severe alcohol problem initially. One hypothesis that incorporates the various interrelationships is that *more* treatment does result in better outcomes, and that cooperative, open clients do better *because* they expose themselves to more treatment.

SUMMARY

In summary, only a small number of variables (of the many analyzed) were found to predict improvement during treatment. Greater improvement tended to be shown by those clients who had more severe alcohol problems initially, were more open about alcohol use, were more likely to use tranquilizers and sleeping pills, were less socially-stable but also less socially-isolated, and were more cooperative and stayed in treatment longer. Aside from these few predictors, the general conclusion is that the initial status of clients entering treatment seems to have very little impact on whether the clients will improve in treatment. Presumably, whether the client improves depends on other factors, including changes in life circumstances due to external events, the client's relationship with the COPA counselor, the client's motivation and readiness to change, the client's ability to understand the effects of substance use, and other aspects of human behavior not measured in the current study.

Chapter 11

Conclusions

The COPA approach to addictions treatment is different from the usual approach to treatment in several important ways:

- outreach–COPA counselors go to the client's home
- lack of confrontation–admitting to having a substance problem is not a necessary part of treatment
- holistic–the overall focus of the COPA approach is on quality of life and maintaining independent living.

Treatment consists of addressing the client's goals, helping the client to understand the role of alcohol or drugs in problems in other life areas, dealing with issues at the client's pace, and helping the client replace the role of alcohol or drugs in his or her life with healthier alternatives. Treatment may include any or all of the following: counseling and crisis intervention with the older substance abuser, advice and counseling for the family of the older substance abuser, and advocacy and coordination with other agencies on the client's behalf. The nature and duration of treatment varies according to the client's needs.

The evaluation and case studies at COPA found that the COPA approach was very effective for engaging clients in treatment, including many clients who would not have accepted or been acceptable for traditional addictions treatment. The COPA program provides a client-centered approach for older people, focused on issues that are relevant to older people. Thus, although the program addresses problems, such as depression, that are common among all ages of substance abusers, the program also addresses problems related to substance abuse and aging, such as activities of daily living.

Case studies of COPA clients indicated at least three "types" of older problem drinkers: the long-term chronic alcohol abuser, older people who developed drinking problems in response to grief, and older drinkers whose cognitive/psychiatric problems appeared to contribute to abusive drinking. A fourth type–drinking with an abusive spouse–was hypothesized, but too few cases were encountered to assess this as a separate type. The general treatment approach tended to vary by client type, with more focus on lifestyle counseling for the chronic drinker, grief counseling and education for the reactive drinker, and a variable approach (depending on the circumstances) for those whose alcohol abuse seemed to be interconnected to cognitive or psychiatric problems.

The evaluation at COPA focused on describing the nature of problems among older substance abusers and assessing the outcomes of treatment at COPA, including the factors that seemed to be associated with improvement during treatment. Since little is currently known about the treatment of older substance abusers, and since the COPA treatment was so different from the traditional approach to addictions treatment, an exploratory approach was used in research at COPA. The evaluation was not only exploratory, but also extensive and comprehensive, in order to learn as much as possible about this innovative approach to treating a long-neglected population of substance abusers.

IMPLICATIONS OF FINDINGS
FROM THE COPA EVALUATION
FOR TREATMENT OF OLDER SUBSTANCE ABUSERS

The COPA research obtained a careful description of the client population. Most of these findings confirmed what was already believed by clinicians who counseled older substance abusers. First, older substance abusers are likely to have somewhat different problems than younger ones. Although the physical and emotional problems experienced by older substance abusers may also be common to younger substance abusers, other problems are more of a reflection of the combination of both substance abuse and aging. In particular, COPA clients appeared to differ from younger addictions treatment populations in terms of the high rate of problems among

COPA clients regarding social isolation, activities of daily living, cognitive functioning, and prescription drug use.

In addition, one of the main goals of the COPA program was to help older substance abusers maintain or recover independent living in the community. The strong association of current drinking with increased impairment in cognitive functioning and self-care supported the premise that reducing alcohol consumption by older alcohol abusers is likely to help these individuals maintain independent community living. This is an important concern in treating the older substance abuser, but rarely a consideration for younger treatment populations.

Unlike traditional treatment programs, the COPA program was prepared to treat (and did treat) persons who were unwilling to acknowledge substance abuse problems. This was reflected in underestimates of alcohol and drug use when using client self-report compared to other sources of information about the client. Another finding of the study was that some clients appeared to experience substantial alcohol-related problems with fairly low consumption levels. This would suggest that even where self-reported consumption levels are valid, consumption data alone may provide unreliable estimates of *alcohol problems*.

In terms of outcomes, the COPA approach seemed to result in at least some improvement for about three-quarters of clients, and improvement tended to be stable over time. Most clients did not become abstinent, and many continued to have some substance-related problems. Nevertheless, most were doing better following treatment at COPA, and some were doing very much better. In an informal follow-up done as part of the case studies, most clients attributed successful outcome to the relationship with the COPA counselor.

The research was able to identify only a few significant predictors of success. In general, those who had more significant alcohol problems initially, those who were more open about problems, and those who were more cooperative in treatment tended to be more likely to improve. Lower social stability and higher use of tranquilizers and sleeping pills also tended to be associated with a greater likelihood of improvement. On the other hand, initial identification of high social isolation indicated a poor prognosis. Considering the many analyses conducted to evaluate predictors of outcome, the most justified conclusion at this time is that the COPA approach seems to be generally applicable for older substance abusers. The research did not identify particular groups who would most likely benefit, nor did it identify particular groups who should be excluded. The program's success with chronic skid row alcohol abusers was particularly noteworthy and hopeful.

Since the founding of the program, increasing interest has been developing in the approach pioneered by Saunders et al. (1992). A number of programs for older people have developed in the past decade using the unusual approach of seeking out and helping persons who are unable to confront their own substance abuse. This approach involves a nondirective orientation to treatment, where the client determines the kind of help he or she can use to address substance-related problems. It seems particularly important that the older person control his or her treatment and not be faced with a younger counselor (who may not understand the client's background or circumstances) deciding what should be done. This orientation to treatment is consistent with recent philosophies of empowerment, and may well prove beneficial for other age groups experiencing problems related to use of alcohol or other drugs.

APPENDICES

APPENDIX A
CLIENT CONTACT RECORD

FILE NO. _____

WORKER: _____

OBSERVER: _____

|__ / __ / __ / __ / __|
Day   Month   Year

LOCATION OF VISIT:

☐☐ Key Code #
☐6 Other _____ Specify

DURATION OF VISIT:

|__|__|__| Minutes

REASON FOR VISIT:

☐1 Regular, or
☐☐ Key Code #, or
☐11 Other _____ Specify

VISIT INITIATED BY:

☐☐ Key Code #, or
☐5 Other _____ Specify

OTHERS PRESENT AT VISIT:
(Key Code # and specify where appropriate for each person present)

☐☐
☐☐
☐☐
☐☐
☐☐

SUMMARY OF CLIENT STATUS:

Health Rating
(0-20 very poor, 21-40 poor, 41-60 major problems, 61-80 minor problems, 81-100 good to ideal)
_____ physical _____ emotional _____ mental
(If rating is less than 81 or if more details required, complete Health Form)

Alcohol Consumption Since Last Contact:
(Check one)
☐1 abstinent
☐2 light
☐3 heavy problem drinking
☐8 not applicable
☐9 no Information
→ (Details on Alcohol form)

Frequency of Drinking According to Client:
(Check one)
☐0 none
☐1 occasional
☐2 frequent (but not daily)
☐3 daily
☐4 some drinking (frequency unknown)
☐8 not applicable
☐9 no Information

|__|__| average number of standard drinks per day

Current Economic Status and Accommodation Status:

ECONOMIC (Check one)	ACCOMMODATION (Check one)
☐1	☐1 no problems
☐2	☐2 slight problems but tolerable
☐3	☐3 somewhat severe
☐4	☐4 very severe
☐8	☐8 not applicable
☐9	☐9 no Information

(Details on Economic and/or Accommodation Forms)

Status of Current Drug Use:
(Check one)
☐1 no problems with drug use
☐2 slight problems with drug use
☐3 moderate problems
☐4 severe problems
☐8 not applicable
☐9 no Information
→ (Details on Drug Form)

Spouse/Significant Other/Cohabitant:
(Check one)
☐0 not applicable, or
☐1 source of client strength
☐2 no problems
☐3 slight problems
☐4 moderate problems
☐5 major problems
☐9 no Information
→ (Details on Spouse Form)

SUMMARY OF CLIENT STATUS:

OTHER AGENCY INVOLVEMENT WITH CLIENT SINCE LAST CONTACT
(Key Code # and specify each agency)

☐
☐
☐
☐

SALIENT FEATURES OF CLIENT DURING CONTACT:

MOOD
anxious	1 2 3 4 5	relaxed
tired	1 2 3 4 5	well-rested
unhappy	1 2 3 4 5	happy
angry	1 2 3 4 5	not angry
frustrated/ upset	1 2 3 4 5	at peace
uncertain	1 2 3 4 5	confident
other:		

ATTITUDE TO COPA WORKER
uncooperative	1 2 3 4 5	cooperative
indifferent	1 2 3 4 5	enthusiastic
passive	1 2 3 4 5	active
defensive	1 2 3 4 5	open

Worker's Opinion of Client's Accuracy in Reporting Frequency and Standard Drinks:

FREQUENCY
(Check one)
☐1
☐2
☐9

STANDARD DRINKS
(Check one)
☐1 accurate report
☐2 under-report
☐2 over-report
☐9 no information

Social Contacts
☐1 no social contacts
☐2 contacts with volunteer/agency only
☐3 limited contacts
☐4 satisfying social contacts
☐9 no information
→ *(Details on Social Contacts Form)*

Leisure Activities
☐1 very inactive
☐2 some activity
☐3 satisfying recreation
☐9 no information
→ *(Details on Leisure Form)*

ADL/Nutrition

	POOR	FAIR	ADE-QUATE	GOOD	EXCEL-LENT	NO INFO
personal hygiene	☐1	☐2	☐3	☐4	☐5	☐9
care of clothing	☐1	☐2	☐3	☐4	☐5	☐9
care of living quarters	☐1	☐2	☐3	☐4	☐5	☐9
adequacy of diet	☐1	☐2	☐3	☐4	☐5	☐9
appetite	☐1	☐2	☐3	☐4	☐5	☐9

→ *(Details on ADL/Nutrition form)*

Current Legal Status:
☐1 no problems
☐2 problems → *(Details on Legal Form)*

SUMMARY OF MAJOR FEATURES OF CONTACT: *(Check all that apply)*
☐1 focus on specific life areas
☐2 general discussion & chit chat
☐3 focus on accomplishing specific tasks with client
☐4 other _____
   (specify)

Appendix B

LESA
Assessment Form

A Structured Interview to Assess the Health Needs of Seniors with a Focus on their Use of Alcohol or other Psychoactive Drugs.

CONFIDENTIAL

LESA
Lifestyle Enrichment
for Senior Adults Program
Centretown Community Health Centre

Note: This assessment is based on an understanding of health as defined by the World Health Organization to be a state of complete physical, mental and social well-being and not merely the absence of disease or infirmity.

© 1992 Centretown Community Health Centre (CCHC)
We welcome you to use the whole or selected parts of this Assessment Form with credit to the LESA Program, Centretown Community Health Centre, Ottawa, Ontario.

Authors' note: This form evolved from assessment procedures done at the Lifestyle Enrichment for Senior Adults Program, with input from the authors of the present project. It is the form currently used at COPA.

LESA Assessment Form

Client ID: _____   Counsellor: _____

Date: _____

THROUGHOUT THE ASSESSMENT
WHERE ONLY YES OR NO ANSWER REQUIRED
CODE FOR *YES = 1* AND *NO = 2*

A. Client Intake

Obtain information directly from client (verbally or by observation)

1. Gender? _____   CODE _____

    1. Male   2. Female

2. Age? _____   CODE _____   Birthdate: __/__/__
                                                                              M D Y

    1. Under 55   4. 75-84
    2. 55-64   5. 85+
    3. 65-74

3. Marital status?_____   CODE _____

    1. Single (never married)   4. Widowed
    2. Married   5. Separated
    3. Common-law   6. Divorced

4. Preferred language _____   CODE _____

    1. English   2. French   3. Other

5. Usual occupation? _____   CODE _____

    1. Professional   5. Unskilled
    2. Managerial or self-employed   6. Homemaker
    3. Skilled (e.g. licensed tradesman, 7. Long-term unemployed
       paraprofessional)   8. Other
    4. Clerical/sales

6. Military?_____ CODE _____

    If YES, years of service_____

7. Source of referral? _____ CODE _____

1	Self	14.	Social service agency
2.	Family	15.	Housing service
3.	Friend or another LESA client	16.	Boarding home
4.	Visiting nurse (VON, PHN, etc)	17.	Group home
5.	Day hospital	18.	Nursing home
6.	General hospital	19.	Retirement home
7.	Family physician	20.	Meals-on-wheels
8.	Private psychiatrist	21.	Visiting homemaker
9.	Psychiatric hospital	22.	Dept. of Veterans Affairs
10.	Detox	23.	Landlord/landlady
11.	Other addictions treatment program	24.	Seniors information service
12.	Police	25.	Seniors activity centre
13.	Legal aid/probation	26.	Other

8. Reason for referral? __ CODE _____

1.	Engagement in treatment	6.	Relapse prevention
2.	Assessment/intervention for alcohol problem	7.	Crisis intervention
3.	Assessment/intervention for drug problem	8.	Support after intensive addiction treatment
4.	Assessment/intervention for alcohol/ drug problem	9.	Other
5.	Assessment/intervention for problem related to alcohol and/or drug use		

9. Employment Status?_____ CODE _____

1.	Employed/self-employed	5.	Unemployed (not disabled)
2.	Homemaker	6.	Disabled (with disability pension)
3.	Student/re-training	7.	Disabled (without pension)
4.	Retired	8.	Other

10. Main Sources of Income?

    Employment _____
    Pension _____
    Savings/Inheritance/Trust Fund _____
    Social Assistance (FBA) _____

Social Assistance (GWA) _____
Family Support _____
Other: _____

Is money a concern for the client?_____ CODE _____

11. Type of accommodation?_____   CODE _____

  1. Own home or condo
  2. Rented home or apartment
  3. Subsidized housing
  4. Rooming house
  5. Shelter/hostel
  6. Group home

  7. Seniors home
  8. Nursing home
  9. Institution
  10. No fixed address
  11. Other

Is accommodation permanent?_____   CODE _____

Do you live with anyone?_____ CODE _____

  1. Live alone
  2. With partner/spouse
  3. With family (no spouse)

  4. With spouse & family
  5. With friend(s)
  6. Group setting

12. Do you presently or have you
    ever smoked?_____   CODE _____

  1. Never smoked
  2. Past smoker

  3. Current smoker

If you currently smoke, number of cigarettes per day?   _____

13. Do you presently drink coffee, tea, or cola?

_____ CODE _____

If YES, number per day: coffee _____ cups
                            tea   _____ cups
                            cola   _____ 8 oz.

14. Do you drink alcoholic beverages?_____CODE _____

If "YES", please estimate how many drinks you consumed during the
past week (begin with the day before the assessment and work backwards).

ONE STANDARD DRINK = 5 OZ. TABLE WINE, 3 OZ. FORTIFIED WINE (SHERRY, APERITIF), 12 OZ. BEER, 1 1/2 OZ. LIQUOR

Sunday _____ Monday _____ Tuesday _____ Wednesday _____
Thursday _____ Friday _____ Saturday_____

B. Physical Health

1. In general, compared to other persons your age would you say your health is_____ CODE _____

   1. Excellent
   2. Very good
   3. Good

   4. Fair
   5. Poor

2. Do you have any of the following medical problems? (Mark with l)

   Heart Disease _____
   High Blood Pressure _____
   Liver Disease _____
   Stomach Problems _____
   TB _____
   Diabetes _____
   Kidney Problems _____
   Stroke/Paralysis _____
   Pancreatitis _____
   Respiratory problem _____

   Hearing Problems _____
   Vision Problems _____
   Chronic Pain _____
   Arthritis/Osteoporosis _____
   Hallucinations _____
   Seizures/Epilepsy _____
   Recent Injury _____
   Sexually Trans. Disease _____
   Over/Under Weight _____
   Other _____

3. Have you had any changes in your health lately?
   _____ CODE _____

   1. Improved some lately
   2. Noticed no change

   3. Worsened some recently
   4. Recently had severe and/or disabling problem

4. Have you been feeling tired?_____ CODE _____

   1. Almost every day
   2. Most days

   3. Some days
   4. No or almost never

5. How are you sleeping at night?_____ CODE _____

   1. Usually get a good night's sleep
   2. Have had some trouble sleeping
   3. Rarely get a good night's sleep

6. Have you been ill with colds, flu, etc.?____   CODE   _____

  1. No or almost never
  2. Occasionally
  3. Frequently

7. During the past 12 months would you describe your life as...
   _____   CODE   _____

  1. Very stressful   3. Not very stressful
  2. Fairly stressful   4. Not at all stressful

8. Most days, do you eat:

   Breakfast   _____
   Lunch   _____
   Dinner   _____

9. Do your eating habits provide a well-balanced intake of food each day
   (contain fruit, vegetables, meat, cereal, etc.)?
   _____   CODE   _____

  1. Eat very little or only one type of food on most days.
  2. Eat well one or two days a week but rarely more
  3. Eat a well-balanced diet most days

10. Are you using vitamin supplements (prescription or non-prescription)?
    _____   CODE   _____

  1. Almost every day   3. Rarely or never
  2. Sometimes

11. Weight status of client._____   CODE   _____

  1. Very overweight (>30%)   4. Moderately underweight
  2. Moderately overweight (10-30%)   (10-20%)
  3. In desirable weight range   5. Very underweight (>20%)

12. Are you currently receiving medical assistance for health problems?
    _____   CODE   _____

   Physician_____   Specialist_____
   Psychiatrist_____   Visiting Nurse_____
   Other:_____

13. Have you been hospitalized in the past six months for a physical illness
    or injury?_____   CODE   _____

14. Do you currently have any physical problems related to the excessive use of alcohol?_____ CODE _____

  1. None
  2. Some
        3. Many

15. What medications (OTC & Prescription) are you presently taking? List:

_____

_____

_____

_____

16. Do you currently have any physical problems related to the excessive use of medications (OTC-prescription) or other drugs?
_____ CODE _____

  1. None
  2. Some
        3. Many

17. How often do you use medications such as tranquilizers, sleeping pills or pain medication?_____ CODE _____

  1. Daily
  2. Nearly every day
  3. 3-4 times a week
  4. 1-2 times a week

  5. 2-3 times a month
  6. About once a month
  7. Less than once a month
  8. Never use medications

18. How long have you used these medications? _____ years and/or _____ months

NOTES ON PHYSICAL HEALTH AND NUTRITION:

C. Mental Health

1. During the past few weeks, how often did you feel . . .

    CODES   1 = Never   2 = Sometimes   3 = Often

    Particularly excited or interested in something? _____
    Proud because someone complimented you on
        something you had done? _____
    On top of the world? _____
    That things were going your way? _____
    Pleased about having accomplished something? _____
    So restless that you couldn't sit long in a chair? _____
    Very lonely or remote from other people? _____
    Depressed or very unhappy? _____
    Upset because someone criticized you? _____
    Bored? _____

2. a) Do you have any of the following concerns?

    CODES   1 = Yes   2 = No   3 = Sometimes/a little

Tension/anxiety	_____	CODE	_____
Eating problems	_____	CODE	_____
Sleeping problems	_____	CODE	_____
Depression/feelings of sadness	_____	CODE	_____
Loneliness	_____	CODE	_____
Feeling afraid/overwhelmed (phobic)	_____	CODE	_____
Feeling frustrated	_____	CODE	_____
Feeling people are against you	_____	CODE	_____
Feeling inferior/inadequate	_____	CODE	_____
Having thoughts/impulses that scare you	_____	CODE	_____
Feeling aggressive or angry	_____	CODE	_____
Having thoughts of suicide	_____	CODE	_____
Not feeling close to people	_____	CODE	_____
Having sexual problems	_____	CODE	_____
Having no energy	_____	CODE	_____

Feeling the loss of someone/
 something important to you   _____   CODE   _____
Feeling worried   _____   CODE   _____
Other emotional problems:
 (specify)_____   _____   CODE   _____

b)   Comments on effects of alcohol/drugs on emotional concerns:

_____

_____

_____

3.   Have you ever received professional help for any of these problems?
_____   CODE   _____

1.   Currently receiving help   3.   Received help in past,
2.   No   but not now

From whom (name & speciality):_____

_____

4.   a) Cognitive problems

Do you have any problems with:

Memory:
 Great difficulty remembering   1 2 3 4 5   Excellent memory

Concentration:
 Very distracted   1 2 3 4 5   Good concentration

Speech:
 Great difficulty speaking   1 2 3 4 5   Fluent and articulate

Do you ever feel:

Confused:
 Very confused   1 2 3 4 5   Very clear thinking

Disoriented:
  Very disoriented   1 2 3 4 5   Well oriented

b) Effects of alcohol/drug use on cognitive problems:

_____

_____

_____

Complete information for substance use that is a major problem for
the client; may include both alcohol and drugs.
CODES
1 = Makes problems worse   2 = No effect   3 = Makes problems better

	Alcohol				Drugs	
Memory	_____	CODE	_____	_____	CODE	_____
Concentration	_____	CODE	_____	_____	CODE	_____
Speech	_____	CODE	_____	_____	CODE	_____
Confusion	_____	CODE	_____	_____	CODE	_____
Orientation	_____	CODE	_____	_____	CODE	_____

5. Have you ever received professional help for any of these problems?

_____CODE _____

1. Currently receiving help   3. Received help in past, but not now
2. No

    From whom (name & speciality):_____

    _____

6. CAGE

    Have you ever felt you should cut down on
    your drinking?   _____CODE_____

Have people annoyed you by criticizing
      your drinking?   _____ CODE _____
Have you ever felt bad or guilty about
      your drinking?   _____ CODE _____
Have you ever had a drink first thing in the morning
      to steady your nerves or get rid of a hangover
      (eye opener)? _____ CODE _____

NOTES ON MENTAL HEALTH:

D. Alcohol Specific (May omit if not applicable)

INTRODUCTION

I am here because_____is concerned about your use
        (the client or referral person)
of alcohol and the effects it may be having on your life. The next
questions are, therefore, related to your alcohol use.

1. How old were you when you started drinking?_____
     CODE_____

  1. Younger than 13 years old   4. 41-55 years
  2. 13-25 years   5. 5+ years
  3. 26-40 years   6. Never drank

2. Are there other people close to you who have had a problem
    with alcohol?

    Spouse/Partner _____   CODE _____
    Children _____   CODE _____
    Mother/Father/Brother/Sister _____   CODE _____
    Current cohabitant (other than
      partner)_____   CODE _____

3. How old were you when drinking first become a concern for you?
    _____   CODE _____

  1. Younger than 13 years old   4. 41-55 years
  2. 13-25 years   5. 55+ years
  3. 26-40 years   6. Not a concern

4. Was this related to something that happened in your life at that time?

    Grief/loss   _____   CODE _____
    Health problems   _____   CODE _____
    Marital/family problems   _____   CODE _____
    Social environment   _____   CODE _____

    Sleep problems   _____   CODE _____
    Job stresses   _____   CODE _____
    Retirement   _____   CODE _____
    Trauma (accident, war
      service)   _____   CODE _____
    Finances   _____   CODE _____

Physical abuse   _____   CODE _____
Sexual abuse   _____   CODE _____
Other: (specify)   _____   CODE _____

5. Were there times in your life when you were drinking more than you are now?_____   CODE_____

    Explain:_____

    _____

6. Were there times in your life when you abstained from drinking?_____
    CODE_____

    If YES, what was the longest period that you abstained? _____ years
    and/or _____ months

    Explain:_____

    _____

7. What is your usual drinking pattern now?_____CODE_____

    1. Never drink
    2. Less than once a month
    3. About once a month
    4. Two or three times a month
    5. One to two times a week
    6. Three to four times a week
    7. Nearly every day
    8. One drink a day
    9. Two drinks a day
    10. Three or more drinks daily
    11. Binge drinking

    Comments:_____

    _____

8. When you are drinking, what is the average number of standard drinks that you usually have per day?

    Reported by client_____ CODE____(# of drinks)
    Reported by other_____ CODE____(# of drinks)

9. Are there days when you drink more than that? If YES, how much?

    Reported by client_____ CODE____(# of drinks)
    Reported by other_____ CODE____(# of drinks)

10. Are you drinking more than you would like? _____ CODE _____
    Do others say you have a problem?_____   CODE _____

11. Let's consider some of the situations when you might feel like drinking.
    (Explore - 1 = Yes,   2 = No)

When you're feeling lonely	_____	Feeling under pressure, tense	_____
Just to be friendly	_____	Feeling out of control	_____
To forget everything	_____	Feeling depressed	_____
To celebrate special occasions	_____	Feeling angry	_____
To relieve pain	_____	Feeling powerless	_____
To cheer me up	_____	To relax	_____
Feeling inadequate	_____	While eating a meal	_____
To help me sleep	_____	Feeling shy	_____
Other (specify):	_____		

12. Alcohol Related Problems

    I'd like to talk to you about some problems that are often associated with
    drinking to discover if you are experiencing any of them.

    I Patterns and direct effects of problem drinking.
    CODES   1=Yes   2=No   3=Client says No, others say Yes

    Injuries or health problems from intoxication   _____
    Delirium tremors   _____
    Vomiting from drinking   _____
    Restless or irritable without a drink   _____
    Excessive sweating after drinking occasions   _____

    Hangover symptoms (including shakiness the day after
      drinking)   _____
    Blackouts while drinking   _____
    Hallucinations after drinking   _____

    Problems controlling amount consumed   _____
    Morning drinking   _____
    Gulping drinks   _____
    Drinking an important part of daily life   _____
    Frequent drinking to intoxication   _____
    Difficulty reducing consumption   _____
    Obsessed with insuring supply   _____

II Social effects of problem drinking.

Current consumption affecting how well client gets along
  with people   _____

Problems with spouse because of drinking   _____

Problems with other family members because
  of drinking   _____

Problems with friends because of drinking   _____

Problems with job (if working) because of drinking   _____

Problems with day-to-day living because of drinking
  (e.g., hygiene, maintaining home)   _____

Arrests because of drinking   _____

Giving up friends because of drinking   _____

Giving up enjoyable activities because of drinking   _____

III Psychological effects of problem drinking.

Current consumption affecting moods   _____

Current consumption affecting memory/ability to think   _____

Feelings of guilt, anger, or depression because
  of drinking   _____

Anxiety or tension because of drinking problem   _____

IV Other effects of problem drinking.

Missing meals or eating too much junk food   _____

Current consumption affecting walking/ability
  to get around   _____

Alcohol related suicide attempts   _____

Health problems from chronic drinking   _____

13. How would you describe your behaviour when drinking?

No change?   _____

Become withdrawn or isolated?   _____

Become more sociable or outgoing?   _____

More argumentative, verbally abusive?   _____
    If YES, who is usual target

_____

Become physically aggressive?   _____
    If YES, who is usual target

_____

Do things in public that others don't like or that you
wouldn't do if sober? _____

If YES, describe

_____

14. Have you previously received treatment for an alcohol problem?

_____ CODE_____

If YES, indicate type of treatment, place, and year:

	WHERE	YEAR	CODE
Detox	_____	_____	_____
Inpatient	_____	_____	_____
Outpatient/day treatment	_____	_____	_____
Drug therapy/ Antabuse/Tempasil	_____	_____	_____
Self-help (eg. AA)	_____	_____	_____
Family physician	_____	_____	_____
Psychiatrist	_____	_____	_____
Other	_____	_____	_____

15. Is your family physician aware of your alcohol use?_____CODE _____

16. How important is it for you to get help now?_____CODE _____

1. Not at all   3. Moderately
2. Slightly   4. Extremely

NOTES ON ALCOHOL USE:

E. Other Drug Use Specific (May omit if not applicable)

I am here because _____ is concerned about your use of
(client or referral agent)

_____ and the effect that it may be having on your life.
 (name substance)

Therefore, the next set of questions are related to your use of drugs/
 medications.

1. Have you taken any of the following medication (either prescribed by
    by your doctor or bought at the pharmacy) in the last 30 days?

    CODES   1=Yes, for use   2=Yes, on prescription   3=Don't use

	CODE
Aspirin or similar pain reliever	____
Tranquillizers such as valium	____
Diet pills or stimulants	____
Anti-depressants	____
Codeine, demerol, morphine	____
Allergy medicine such as sinutab	____
Cough or cold remedies	____
Penicillin or similar antiobiotic	____
Heart or blood pressure medicine	____
Insulin or similar diabetic medication	____
Sleeping pills	____
Stomach remedies or laxatives	____
Other medications: (specify)	____

---

2. I would like to talk to you a little more about the drugs you have taken
    in the last 30 days. (Counsellor to recopy medications from #B-15.
    This question includes more detail about usage.)

    CODES: Treatment Compliance
        1 = As prescribed   3 = Less than prescribed
        2 = More than prescribed   4 = Erratic

MEDICATION NAME	DOSAGE	DURATION	TREATMENT COMPLIANCE
_____	_____	_____	_____
_____	_____	_____	_____
_____	_____	_____	_____
_____	_____	_____	_____
_____	_____	_____	_____
_____	_____	_____	_____

3. Indicate misuse/abuse of non-psychoactive drugs_____   CODE_____

4. Do you take all of your medications/drugs by mouth?_____   CODE_____

5. Are these drugs being prescribed by more than one physician?_____   CODE_____

   If YES, explain_____

   _____

6. Have you ever used any of the following?
   CODES 1 = Has taken drug   2 = Used in last 30 days   3= Never taken

Marijuana or hash	_____	CODE	_____
Cocaine or crack	_____	CODE	_____
LSD	_____	CODE	_____
Speed/amphetamines	_____	CODE	_____
Heroin	_____	CODE	_____

7. Is your drug use a concern for you? _____   CODE_____

    CODE 1 = Yes, client reports a concern.
         2 = Client reports no problem (no contradictory evidence from
             other sources).
         3 = Client reports no problem (other evidence indicates
             a problem).

8. When you started taking _____, was it related to something
                            (name drug)
    that happened in your life at that time?

Grief/loss	_____	CODE	_____
Health problems	_____	CODE	_____
Marital/family problems	_____	CODE	_____
Social environment	_____	CODE	_____
Sleep problems	_____	CODE	_____
Job stresses	_____	CODE	_____
Retirement	_____	CODE	_____
Trauma (accident, war services)	_____	CODE	_____
Finances	_____	CODE	_____
Physical abuse	_____	CODE	_____
Sexual abuse	_____	CODE	_____
Other	_____	CODE	_____

9. Let's consider some of the reasons why you are presently taking
    _____:
           (name drug)

	CODE
Feeling lonely	_____
Feeling under pressure, tense	_____
Feeling afraid	_____
Feeling out of control	_____
Feeling uncomfortable in social situations	_____
To forget everything	_____
Feeling depressed	_____
Feeling helpless	_____
Feeling angry	_____
To relieve pain	_____
To sleep	_____
Because the doctor prescribed them	_____

Because I can't get through the day
  without them   _____

10. I'd like to talk to you about some of the problems that are often associated
    with medication use. (Clarify that this includes all psychoactive/mood
    altering drugs both prescription and OTC). Are you having any concerns in
    the following areas?

Cognitive   CODE

Memory problems/forgetful   _____
Can't concentrate, can't think   _____
Confused   _____
Blackouts   _____

Emotional

Feeling anxious   _____
Feeling tearful, vulnerable   _____
Feeling panicky, afraid to go out   _____
Feeling paranoid   _____

Feeling irritable, angry   _____
Feeling depressed   _____
Feeling suicidal   _____
Having mood swings   _____

Physical

Feeling restless, jittery   _____
Feeling tired, no energy   _____
Unsteady, stumbling, falling, dropping things   _____
Slurred speech   _____
Dry mouth   _____
Headache, dizziness, seeing double   _____
Buzzing, ringing in ears   _____
Less interest in sex   _____

Other

Concern about availability, doctor
  shopping   _____
Need more to have same effect   _____

Problems with spouse, family because of
medication use _____

Problems with friends because of medication
use _____

Problems with day-to-day living (maintaining
home, hygiene) _____

11. If you <u>don't</u> take your medication, what happens to you?

Change in mood _____ CODE _____
Change in behaviour _____ CODE _____
Change in mental state _____ CODE _____
Change in physical state _____ CODE _____

Describe what happens if you don't take your medication: _____

_____

_____

12. Has anyone ever expressed concern to you about your use of medication?

_____ CODE _____

If YES, who and what concern? _____

_____

13. Is your family physician aware of your use of drugs/medications? _____
CODE _____

14. Have you previously received treatment for problems with
medication/drugs?

_____ CODE _____

If YES, indicate type of treatment, place, and year: _____

	WHERE	YEAR	CODE
Detox	____	____	____
Inpatient	____	____	____
Outpatient/day treatment	____	____	____
Drug therapy/Antabuse/ Tempasil	____	____	____

Self-help (eg. NA)   _____ _____ _____
Family physician   _____ _____ _____
Psychiatrist   _____ _____ _____
Other   _____ _____ _____

15. How important is it for you to get help now?_____ CODE_____

    1.   Not at all   3.   Moderately
    2.   Slightly   4.   Extremely

NOTES ON DRUG USE:

F. Problems of Daily Living

1. a) How are you managing with:

SCALE:	Very poorly					Very well
Personal hygiene	1	2	3	4	5	
Care of clothing	1	2	3	4	5	
Care of living quarters	1	2	3	4	5	
Food preparation	1	2	3	4	5	
Use of telephone	1	2	3	4	5	
Shopping	1	2	3	4	5	
Banking	1	2	3	4	5	
Using transportation	1	2	3	4	5	
Diet	1	2	3	4	5	
Exercise	1	2	3	4	5	

b) Effects of alcohol/drug use on daily living:
Complete information for substance use that is a major problem for
the client; may include both alcohol and drugs.
CODES 1 = Makes problems worse 2 = No effect 3 = Makes problems better

	ALCOHOL	DRUGS
Personal hygiene	_____	_____
Care of clothing	_____	_____
Care of living quarters	_____	_____
Food preparation	_____	_____
Use of telephone	_____	_____
Shopping	_____	_____
Banking	_____	_____
Using transportation	_____	_____
Diet	_____	_____
Exercise	_____	_____

Notes on Effects of Alcohol/Drug Use on Daily Living:

_____

_____

c) Do you need help with any of these activities?
CODES   1 = Yes   2 = No   3 = Receiving Help

Personal hygiene	CODE	_____
Care of clothing	CODE	_____
Care of living quarters	CODE	_____
Food preparation	CODE	_____
Use of telephone	CODE	_____
Shopping	CODE	_____
Banking	CODE	_____
Using transportation	CODE	_____
Diet	CODE	_____
Exercise	CODE	_____

G. LESA Workers Assessment

1. During the past 5 years, has the client been diagnosed/treated by a psychiatrist, psychologist, or other qualified person for any of the following psychiatric disorders?

CODES 1 = Yes   2 = No   3 = Unknown

Organic mental disorder	_____	CODE	_____
Psychoactive substance use disorder	_____	CODE	_____
Schizophrenia	_____	CODE	_____
Delusional (paranoid) disorder	_____	CODE	_____
Mood disorders (including bipolar disorder and major depression)	_____	CODE	_____
Anxiety disorders	_____	CODE	_____
Somatoform disorders	_____	CODE	_____
Dissociative disorders	_____	CODE	_____
Sexual disorders	_____	CODE	_____
Sleep disorders	_____	CODE	_____
Personality disorders	_____	CODE	_____
Other disorders (specify)	_____	CODE	_____

NOTES:

2.	Observations of client during assessment.

On a scale of 1 to 10 (1 being low, 10 being high), choose an appropriate number to describe the client during assessment interview(s).

Orientation
Very disoriented	1 2 3 4 5 6 7 8 9 10		Well-oriented

Memory:
Great difficulty	1 2 3 4 5 6 7 8 9 10		Excellent memory
remembering

Speech:
  Great difficulty   1 2 3 4 5 6 7 8 9 10   Fluent and articulate
    speaking

Mood:
  Very sad   1 2 3 4 5 6 7 8 9 10   Very happy

Energy Level:
  Very lethargic   1 2 3 4 5 6 7 8 9 10   Very energetic

Concentration:
  Very distracted   1 2 3 4 5 6 7 8 9 10   Good concentration

Rationality:
  Irrational   1 2 3 4 5 6 7 8 9 10   Completely rational

Paranoia:
  Very paranoid   1 2 3 4 5 6 7 8 9 10   Not at all paranoid

Confusion:
  Very confused   1 2 3 4 5 6 7 8 9 10   Very clear thinking

3. Do you believe that the client is under-reporting alcohol consumption?

    _____ CODE _____

4. Does the client deny excessive use, when there is evidence that the client *is* consuming alcohol excessively?_____CODE_____

  1. No evidence that client consumes   3. Some denial
     alcohol excessively
  2. No denial   4. Strong denial

5. Does the client deny negative consequences of alcohol use, when there is clear evidence of negative consequences? _____ CODE_____

  1. No evidence that client consumes   3. Some denial
     alcohol excessively
  2. No denial   4. Strong denial

6. Level of current alcohol problem.

  According to client:_____ CODE _____
  According to other source:_____ CODE _____
  According to worker:_____ CODE _____

  1. Severe problem   4. Client drinks but has
  2. Moderate problem   no problem
  3. Slight problem   5. Client is abstinent

7. Pattern of alcohol consumption.

According to client:_____   CODE _____
According to other source:_____   CODE _____
According to worker:_____   CODE _____

1. Binge (intoxicated for whole day at least two days in a row)	5. Intermittent moderate/ binge
2. Heavy (5+ drinks in one day or intoxicated)	6. Light (max. 2 drinks daily)
3. Both binge and heavy	7. Intermittent light/binge or heavy
4. Moderate (max. 4 drinks daily, never intoxicated)	8. Intermittent light/moderate
	9. Abstinent

8. Were there any signs of alcohol use during previous 24 hours?_____   CODE _____

9. Do you believe that the client is under-reporting psychoactive drug use? _____   CODE _____

10. Client's status regarding non-prescription drug use.

Severe Problem   1 2 3 4 5 6 7 8 9 10   No problems

11. Client's status regarding prescription drug use.

Severe Problem   1 2 3 4 5 6 7 8 9 10   No problems

12. Nature of current drug problem:

CODE 1 IF CLIENT IS EXPERIENCING THE PROBLEM

Taking too much   CODE _____
Taking too little   CODE _____
Drugs not having desired effect   CODE _____
Side effects from drugs   CODE _____
Drug addiction   CODE _____
Alcohol-drug interactions   CODE _____
Cost of drugs   CODE _____
Other drug problems (specify):   CODE _____

_____

13. What is your professional judgement about the client's attitude toward treatment for his or her drinking/drug problem?

Evasive _____ CODE _____
Blaming _____ CODE _____
Putting up a "front" _____ CODE _____
Defeatist _____ CODE _____

Lack of personal responsibility _____ CODE _____
Inability to associate problems
  with use of alcohol or drugs _____ CODE _____
Unable to consider options _____ CODE _____
Manipulative _____ CODE _____

Seeking help _____ CODE _____
Open _____ CODE _____
Realistic _____ CODE _____
Very committed to resolving
  problems _____ CODE _____

14. Presenting Problems:

CODE 1 FOR EACH PRESENTING PROBLEM IDENTIFIED

Accommodation _____ Developmentally handicapped _____
Marital/family _____ Mental health problems _____
Employment _____ Mental illness _____
Financial _____ Physical health problems _____
Leisure _____ Physical disability _____
 Social health problems _____

Substance abuse
Alcohol & drugs _____ Legal _____
Alcohol only _____ Physical abuse _____
Drugs only _____ Sexual abuse _____
By significant other _____ Other: (specify) _____
_____

COMMENTS REGARDING PRESENTING PROBLEMS:

15. Major problem substance(s) for client.

CODES   1 = Alcohol only   3 = Drugs only
                     2 = Alcohol & drugs   4 = None

   a) Identified in the reason for referral by client or referring agent?
   _____   CODE _____

   b) Identified during intake interview?_____CODE _____

16. Date assessment completed ___ / ___ / ___
                                M   D   Y

17. Number of contacts with the client before assessment completed:_____

18. Worker who completed assessment:_____
                                              (Name)

19. Client accepted?_____   CODE _____

GENERAL COMMENTS:

References

Adams, W. L., Garry, P. J., Rhyne, R., Hunt, W. C., & Goodwin, J. S. (1990). Alcohol intake in the healthy elderly: Changes with age in a cross-sectional and longitudinal study. *Journal of the American Geriatrics Society, 38,* 211-216.

Adlaf, E.M., Smart, R.G., & Jansen, V.A. (1989). *Alcohol use, drug use and well-being among a sample of older adults in Toronto: Preliminary report.* Toronto: Addiction Research Foundation.

Atkinson, R.M. (1984). Substance use and abuse in late life. In R.M. Atkinson (Ed.), *Alcohol and drug abuse in old age* (pp. 1-21). Washington, DC: American Psychiatric Press.

Atkinson, R.M., Ganzini, L., & Bernstein, M.J. (1992). Alcohol and substance-use disorders in the elderly. In *Handbook of Mental Health and Aging* (2nd Edition) (pp. 515-555). New York: Academic Press.

Atkinson, R.M., Turner, J.A., Kofoed, L.L., & Tolson, R.L. (1985). Early versus late onset alcoholism in older persons: Preliminary findings. *Alcoholism: Clinical and Experimental Research, 9*(6), 513-515.

Babor, T.F., & Dolinksy, Z.S. (1988). Alcoholic typologies: Historical evolution and empirical evaluation of some common classification schemes (pp. 245-266). In R.M. Rose & J. Barrett (Eds.), *Alcoholism: Origins and outcome.* New York: Raven Press.

Barnes, G.M. (1982). Patterns of alcohol use and abuse among older persons in a household population. In W.G. Wood, M.F. Elias, R.C. Adelman, & G.S. Roth (Eds.), *Alcoholism and aging: Advances in research* (pp. 3-15). Boca Raton, Florida: CRC Press, Inc.

Blazer, D., George, L., Woodbury, M., Manton, K., & Jordan, K. (1984). The elderly alcoholic: A profile. In G. Maddox, L.N. Robins, & N. Rosenberg (Eds.), *Nature and extent of alcohol problems among the elderly* (pp. 275-297). (Research Monograph No. 14.) Rockville, Maryland: NIAAA.

Brown, B.B. & Chiang, C.P. (1983-84). Drug and alcohol abuse among the elderly: Is being alone the key? *International Journal of Aging and Human Development, 18*(1), 1-12.

Busby, W. J., Campbell, A. J., Borrie, M. J., & Spears, G. F. S. (1988). Alcohol use in a community-based sample of subjects aged 70 years and older. *Journal of the American Geriatrics Society, 36,* 301-305.

Carruth, B. (1973). Life styles, drinking practices and drinking problems of older Americans. In E.P. Williams et al., *Alcoholism and problem drinking among older persons* (pp. 67-109). Final report to the Administration on Aging, Department of Health, Education and Welfare, Washington, DC.

Carstensen, L. L., Rychtarik, R. G., & Prue, D. M. (1985). Behavioral treatment of the geriatric alcohol abuser: A long term follow-up study. *Addictive Behaviors: An International Journal, 10*, 307-311.

Clark, W.B., & Midanik, L., (1982). Alcohol use and alcohol problems among U.S. adults: Results of the 1979 National Survey. In *Alcohol and Health Monograph No. 1: Alcohol consumption and related problems*. Rockville, Maryland: National Institute on Alcohol Abuse and Alcoholism.

Community Older Persons Alcohol Program. (1992). *COPA program description*. Toronto: COPA program.

Droller, H. (1964). Some aspects of alcoholism in the elderly. *The Lancet*, 137-139.

Duckworth, G. L., & Rosenblatt, A. (1976). Helping the Elderly Alcoholic. *Social Casework: The Journal of Contemporary Social Work, 57*, 291-301.

Dupree, L.W., Broskowski, H., & Schonfeld, L. (1984). The gerontology alcohol project: A behavioral treatment program for elderly alcohol abusers. *The Gerontologist, 24*(5), 510-516.

Edwards, G., Brown, D., Oppenheimer, E., Sheehan, M., Taylor, C., & Duckitt, A. (1988). Long term outcome for patients with drinking problems: The search for predictors. *British Journal of Addiction, 83*, 917-927.

Finney, J.W. & Moos, R.H. (1984). Life stressors and problem drinking among older adults. In M. Galanter (Ed.), *Recent developments in alcoholism, Vol. 2*. New York: Plenum Press.

Finney, J.W., Moos, R.H., & Chan, D.A. (1981). Length of stay and program component effects in the treatment of alcoholism: A comparison of two techniques for process analyses. *Journal of Consulting and Clinical Psychology, 49*(1), 120-131.

Folstein, M.F., Folstein, S.E., & McHugh, P.R. (1975). "Mini-mental state." A practical method for grading the cognitive state of patients for the clinician. *Journal of Psychiatric Research, 12*, 189-198.

Giordano, J.A. & Beckham, K. (1985). Alcohol use and abuse in old age: An examination of Type II alcoholism. *Journal of Gerontological Social Work, 9*(1), 65-83.

Glynn, R.J., Bouchard, G.R., LoCastro, J.S., & Hermos, J.A. (1984). Changes in alcohol consumption behaviors among men in the normative aging study. In G. Maddox, L.N. Robins, & N. Rosenberg (Eds.). *Nature and extent of alcohol problems among the elderly* (pp. 101-116). (Research Monograph No. 14.) Rockville, Maryland: National Institute on Alcohol Abuse and Alcoholism.

Gomberg, E. (1982). *Alcohol use and alcohol problems among the elderly*. (Alcohol and Health Monograph No. 4.) U.S. Department of Health and Human Services. Rockville, Maryland.

Graham, K. (1986). Identifying and measuring alcohol abuse among the elderly. Serious problems with existing instrumentation. *Journal of Studies on Alcohol, 47*(4), 322-326.

Graham, K. (1987). *Inter-rater reliability of data collection measures for the evaluation of the COPA Project*. Report provided to the COPA Project.

Graham, K., & Ekdahl, A. (1986). *Addiction prone*. Toronto: Addiction Research Foundation.

Graham, K., & Timney, C. (1985, October). *The evaluator as empathic mind probe and graphic artist*. Paper presented at a Joint Meeting of the Canadian Evaluation Society, Evaluation Network, and the Evaluation Research Society, Toronto, Ontario.

Graham, K., Birchmore Timney, C., & White-Campbell, M. (1990). *COPA case management study*. Unpublished manuscript available from author.

Graham, K., Saunders, S.J., & Flower, M. (1990). Approaches and agenda of researchers or evaluators versus those of community developers: Perspectives of the program developer, the program manager, and the program evaluator. In N. Giesbrecht, P. Conley, R.W. Denniston, L. Gliksman, H. Holder, A. Pederson, R. Room, & M. Shain (Eds.), *Research, action, and the community: Experiences in the prevention of alcohol and other drug problems.* (OSAP Prevention Monograph No. 4.) Rockville, Maryland: Office for Substance Abuse Prevention.

Graham, K., Zeidman, A., Flower, M.C., Saunders, S.J., & White-Campbell, M. (1989, August). *Case study analyses of elderly persons who have alcohol problems*. Final report to NHRDP. (Project No. 6606-3414-43DA.) London, Ontario: Addiction Research Foundation (Evaluation Dept.)

Graham K., Zeidman, A., Flower, M.C., Saunders, S.J., & White-Campbell, M. (1992). A typology of elderly persons with alcohol problems. *Alcoholism Treatment Quarterly, 9*(3/4), 79-95.

Hanson, M. (1988). Involving clients in alcoholism outpatient treatment: Implications for social work practice. *Alcoholism Treatment Quarterly, 5*, 209-220.

Health and Welfare Canada (1990). *National alcohol and drug survey (1989): Highlights report.* (Cat. No. #39-175/1990E.) Ottawa: Minister of Supply and Services, Canada.

Helzer, J.E., Carey, K.E., & Miller, R.H. (1984). Predictors and correlates of recovery in older versus younger alcoholics. In G. Maddox, L.N. Robins, and N. Rosenberg (Eds.), *Nature and extent of alcohol problems among the elderly* (pp. 83-99). (Research Monograph No. 14). Rockville, Maryland: National Institute on Alcohol Abuse and Alcoholism.

Hilton, M.E. (1988). The demographic distribution of drinking patterns in 1984. *Drug and Alcohol Dependence, 22*, 37-47.

Hinrichsen, J.J. (1984). Toward improving treatment services for alcoholics of advanced age. *Alcohol Health and Research World, 8*(3), 31-39.

Hubbard, R.W., Santos, J.F., & Santos, M.A. (1979, March). Alcohol and older adults: Overt and covert influences. *Social Casework: The Journal of Contemporary Social Work*, 166-170.

Israelstam, S. (1988). Psychosocial factors in excessive drinking of senior citizens and the general population: Opinions of alcohol intervention workers. *Psychological Reports, 62*, 80-82.

Jellinek, E.M. (1960). *The disease concept of alcoholism*. New Haven, Connecticut: Hillhouse Press.

Kafetz, K., & Cox, M. (1982). Alcohol excess and the Senile Squalor Syndrome. *Journal of the American Geriatrics Society, 30*(U), 706.

Kofoed, L. L., Tolson, R. L., Atkinson, R. M., Toth, R. L., & Turner, J. A. (1987). Treatment compliance of older alcoholics: An elder-specific approach is superior to "mainstreaming." *Journal of Studies on Alcohol, 48*, 47-51.

Kozma, A., Stones, M.J., & McNeil, J.K. (1991). *Psychological well-being in later life*. Toronto, Canada: Butterworths.

Lindesay, J., Briggs, K., & Murphy, E. (1989). The Guy's/Age Concern Survey prevalence rates of cognitive impairment, depression and anxiety in an urban elderly community. *British Journal of Psychiatry, 155*, 317-329.

Linn, M.W. (1978). Attrition of older alcoholics from treatment. *Addictive Diseases: An International Journal, 3*(3), 437-447.

McKim, W.A., & Mishara, B.L. (1987). *Drugs and Aging*. Toronto: Butterworths.

Meyer, R.E., Babor, T.F., & Mirkin, P.M. (1983). Typologies in alcoholism: An overview. *The International Journal of the Addictions, 18*(2), 235-249.

Meyers, A.R., Hingson, R., Mucatel, M., & Goldman, E. (1982). Social and psychologic correlates of problem drinking in old age. *Journal of the American Geriatrics Society, 30*(7), 452-456.

Miller, W.R. & Hester, R.K. (1980). Treating the problem drinker: Modern approaches. In W. Miller (Ed.), *The Addictive Behaviors*. Pergamon Press.

Miller, W.R. & Hester, R.K. (1986). The effectiveness of alcoholism treatment: What research reveals (pp. 121-174). In W.R. Miller & N. Heather (Eds.), *Treating addictive behaviors: Processes of change*. New York: Plenum Press.

Mishara, B.L. & Kastenbaum, R. (1980). *Alcohol and Old Age*. New York: Grune and Stratton.

Morey, L.C., Skinner, H.A., & Blashfield, R.K. (1984). A typology of alcohol abusers: Correlates and implications. *Journal of Abnormal Psychology, 93*(4), 408-417.

Nakamura, C.M., Molgaard, C.A., Stanford, E.P., Peddecord, K.M., Morton, D.J., Lockery, S.A., Zuniga, M., & Gardner, L.D. (1990). A discriminant analysis of severe alcohol consumption among older persons. *Alcohol and Alcoholism, 25*(1), 75-80.

Ogborne, A.C. (1978). Patient characteristics as predictors of treatment outcomes for alcohol and drug abusers. In Y. Israel, F.B. Glaser, H. Kalant, R.E. Popham, W. Schmidt, & R.G. Smart, *Research advances in alcohol and drug problems, Vol. 4*. New York: Plenum.

Rathbone-McCuan, E. (1982). Health and social intervention issues with the older alcoholic and alcohol abuser. In W.G. Wood, M.F. Elias, R.C. Adelman, & G.S. Roth (Eds.), *Alcoholism and aging: Advances in research*. Boca Raton, Florida: CRC Press.

Rathbone-McCuan, E. & Bland, J. (1975). A treatment typology for the elderly alcohol abuser. *Journal of the American Geriatrics Society, 23*, 553-557.

Rathbone-McCuan, E., Lohn, H., Levenson, J., & Hsu, J. (1976). *Community survey of aged alcoholics and problem drinkers*. Baltimore, Maryland: The Levindale Geriatric Research Center.

Rosin, A.J. & Glatt, M.M. (1971). Alcohol excess in the elderly. *Quarterly Journal of Studies on Alcohol, 32*, 53-59.

Rush, B. & Timney, C. (1983, July/Aug). The detection and assessment of alcohol-related problems in health and social service agencies. *Canadian Journal of Public Health, 74*, 270-275.

Rush, B. & Tyas, S. (1990). Trends in the development of alcohol/drug treatment services in Ontario, 1979-1989. London, Ontario: Addiction Research Foundation.

Rush, B.R. & Ekdahl, A. (1987). *Treatment services for alcohol and drug abuse in Ontario: Results of a provincial survey.* Toronto: Addiction Research Foundation.

Saunders, S.J., Graham, K., Flower, M.C., & Shea, J.P. (1985). *Community older persons alcohol project: Assessment form.* (Internal Document No. 58.) Toronto, Ontario: Addiction Research Foundation.

Saunders, S.J., Graham, K., Flower, M., & White-Campbell, M. (1992). The COPA project as a model for the management of early dementia in the community. In G.M.M. Jones & B.M.L. Miesen (Eds.), *Care-giving in dementia.* New York: Tavistock/Routledge.

Schonfeld, L. & Dupree, L. W. (1990). Older problem drinkers–long-term and late-life onset abusers: What triggers their drinking? *Aging*, 5-8.

Schuckit, M.A., Morrissey, E.R., & O'Leary, M.R. (1978). Alcohol problems in elderly men and women. *Addictive Diseases: An International Journal, 3*(3), 405-416.

Segovia, J., Bartlett, R.F., & Edwards, A.C. (1989). An empirical analysis of the dimensions of health status measures. *Social Science Medicine, 29*(6), 761-768.

Smart R.G. & Adlaf, E.M. (1987). *Alcohol and other drug use among Ontario adults 1977-1987.* Toronto: Addiction Research Foundation.

Statistics Canada (1987). *General social survey analysis series, Health & Social Support 1985.* (Cat. No. 11-612, No. 1.) Ottawa: Minister of Supply and Services Canada.

Temple, M. T. & Leino, E. V. (1989). Long-Term Outcomes of Drinking: A 20-year longitudinal study of men. *British Journal of Addiction, 84*, 889-899.

Valanis, B., Yeaworth, R. C., & Resing Mullis, M. (1987). Alcohol use among bereaved and nonbereaved older persons. *Journal of Gerontological Nursing, 13*, 26-32.

Van de Vyvere, B., Hughes, M., & Fish, D.G. (1976). The elderly chronic alcoholic: A practical approach. *Canadian Welfare, 2*, 9-13.

Vermette, G., & Létourneau, G. (1990). *Entre la souffrance & l'espoir . . . Étude et analyse d'un mode d'intervention sociale caractérisé par l'action bénévole auprès d'une clientèle âgée toxicomane. Rapport final.* Montréal, Québec: Groupe Harmonie.

Warheit, G.L. & Auth, J.G. (1984). The mental health and social correlates of alcohol use among differing life cycles groups. In G. Maddox, L.N. Robins, &

N. Rosenberg (Eds.), *Nature and extent of alcohol problems among the elderly* (pp. 29-82). (Research Monograph No. 14.) NIAAA, Rockville, Maryland.

Weins, A.N., Menustik, C.E., Miller, S.I., & Schmitz, R.E. (1982-83). Medical-behavioral treatment of the older alcoholic patient. *American Journal of Drug and Alcohol Abuse, 9*(4), 461-475.

Williams, M. (1984). Alcohol and the elderly: An overview. *Alcohol Health Research World, 8*(3), 3-9.

Zimberg, S. (1978a). Diagnosis and treatment of the elderly alcoholic. *Alcoholism: Clinical and Experimental Research, 2,* 27-29.

Zimberg, S. (1978b). Treatment of the elderly alcoholic in the community and in an institutional setting. *Addictive Diseases: An International Journal, 3,* 417-427.

Index